LIFE WORLD LIBRARY

THE LOW COUNTRIES

OTHER BOOKS BY THE EDITORS OF LIFE

LIFE WORLD LIBRARY

THE LOW COUNTRIES

by Eugene Rachlis

and The Editors of LIFE

A STONEHENGE BOOK

TIME INCORPORATED   NEW YORK

COVER: Carrying brave flags
emblazoned with the ancient arms
of their cities, Belgians
march through the streets of Tournai
during a religious festival.

ABOUT THE WRITER

Eugene Rachlis, author of the interpretive text for this volume in the LIFE World Library, is an American journalist of wide experience who first came to know the Low Countries as information officer of the Marshall Plan mission to the Netherlands in 1949 and 1950. Subsequently he served in Paris for four years as chief of operations for the entire Marshall Plan information program, making frequent trips to the Low Countries. Mr. Rachlis began his editorial career before World War II as a reporter for International News Service. After the war he was successively Washington correspondent for the Chicago *Sun*, associate editor of *Kiplinger Magazine*, an editor of *The New York Times Sunday Magazine*, an associate editor of *Collier's* and managing editor of the *Woman's Home Companion*. In addition to his magazine work, he has published a number of books, including *They Came to Kill*, an account of a Nazi sabotage effort in the United States during World War II.

Contents

TIME INC. BOOK DIVISION

EDITOR

Norman P. Ross

COPY DIRECTOR   ART DIRECTOR

William Jay Gold   *Edward A. Hamilton*

CHIEF OF RESEARCH

Beatrice T. Dobie

EDITORIAL STAFF FOR "THE LOW COUNTRIES"

EDITOR, LIFE WORLD LIBRARY	*Oliver E. Allen*
ASSISTANT EDITOR	*Jay Brennan*
DESIGNER	*Ben Schultz*
CHIEF RESEARCHER	*Grace Brynolson*
RESEARCHERS	*Henriette Roosenburg, Irene Ertugrul,*
	Edward Brash, Helen R. Turvey,
	Ava Weekes
PICTURE RESEARCHERS	*Margaret K. Goldsmith,*
	Mary Elizabeth Davidson, Joan T. Lynch
ART ASSOCIATE	*Robert L. Young*
ART ASSISTANTS	*James D. Smith, William Gedney*
COPY STAFF	*Marian Gordon Goldman,*
	Carol Henderson, Dolores A. Littles
PUBLISHER	*Jerome S. Hardy*
GENERAL MANAGER	*John A. Watters*

LIFE MAGAZINE

EDITOR   MANAGING EDITOR   PUBLISHER

Edward K. Thompson   *George P. Hunt*   *C. D. Jackson*

The text for the chapters of this book was written by Eugene Rachlis, the picture essays by David S. Thomson. Valuable help in preparing the book was provided by the following members of Time Inc.: Larry Burrows, Yale Joel, Dmitri Kessel and Stan Wayman, LIFE staff photographers; Farrell Grehan, contributing photographer; Doris O'Neil, Chief, LIFE Picture Library; Clara Applegate, TIME-LIFE News Service; and Content Peckham, Chief, Bureau of Editorial Reference.

Introduction

Would the United States have survived what was probably the lowest point in its history, if the Dutch had not come to its assistance with financial aid? The 13 colonies had been fighting an uphill battle for four years, and they were broke. The revolution had not been going well. Military defeats in the south had paralleled Benedict Arnold's defection to the British, and the morale of the unpaid, disheveled Continental Army had reached a low ebb. Congress was becoming desperate.

To the Dutch bankers of Amsterdam, a loan to the 13 states did not seem a very good risk. To John Adams, who had been sent across the Atlantic to plead for aid, goes the credit for completely reversing this attitude. In February of 1782, the Council of Friesland voted to recognize the "XIII Vereenigde Staaten." The other provinces of the Netherlands rapidly fell in line, and the Dutch bankers of Amsterdam made the first of a series of loans which helped to carry the United States through the critical early years of independence. This Marshall aid in reverse was instrumental in establishing U.S. credit abroad, and it created a bond between the United States and the Low Countries which has continued to develop and flower over the intervening years.

If John Adams were to read this book today, he would approve, for he would find many of his own observations and comments about the people, the customs, the culture and the heritage of the Low Countries just as sound now as when he wrote his diaries in Amsterdam. Eugene Rachlis has effectively and genuinely captured the spirit and the feeling, the historical background and the present atmosphere of these diverse peoples who are crammed into a small area, but who, as he points out, find that there is strength in their diversity.

The courage and determination of the people of the Low Countries have been unfaltering, despite the centuries of floods and military conquests, the almost never-ending shifts in political domination, the breakup and loss of their vast colonial empires, and the destruction caused by two world wars fought over their prostrate lands. The reincarnation of Rotterdam, the dramatic concept of Benelux, the participation in the Coal and Steel Community, and the leadership in the establishment of the Common Market are just a few manifestations of the fact that these people have maintained a forward sense of direction, a belief in themselves, and a confidence in the future that nothing can daunt. Perhaps the kaleidoscopic history of these countries has developed an adaptability to change that has stood them in good stead.

The Editors of LIFE and Mr. Rachlis are to be commended for the preparation of this volume which, whether it be read for pleasure or made the subject of serious study, provides in words and picture essays a penetrating analysis and reflection of the Low Countries against a perceptive historical backdrop.

PHILIP YOUNG
former U.S. Ambassador to the Netherlands

Automobiles share a street in the old Dutch town of Leyden with whizzing cyclists, who are omnipresent in Holland and Belgium.

The windmill is one of many that still decorate the Dutch scene.

1

A Unity through Diversity

SENSITIVE Dutchmen, Belgians and Luxembourgers cringe at the persistent popular image of the Low Countries as quaintly photogenic lands where wooden shoes are standard footwear and tulips blossom in the shadow of slowly turning windmills; where milk is delivered in dogcarts and folk festivals provide a pleasant carnival air; and where medieval castles add a fairy-tale touch. They would rather have their homelands seen as dynamic industrial nations, fully recovered from war and occupation and the loss of lucrative colonies, leading modern Europe toward the hitherto elusive goal of economic and political union. But factories, ports and mines, however dramatic, have never ranked high as tourist attractions, and since tourism is big business in Holland, Belgium and Luxembourg, the anachronistic quaintness is encouraged. Casual visitors to the Low Countries are more likely to remember windmills, whose major function these days is decorative, than they are auto

9

license plates with the letters EUR to identify employees of the European Common Market, which has its headquarters in Brussels.

This is unfortunate, but the Dutch, Belgians and Luxembourgers are themselves partly responsible. The Dutch, for example, view with emotions ranging from good-humored tolerance to downright indignation the American fiction of the boy who put his finger in a hole in a dike and thus saved Holland from flooding devastation. The story was first told by Mary Mapes Dodge, a 19th Century American writer, in *Hans Brinker, or The Silver Skates*, a book whose influence on impressionable minds could well form the basis for a Ph.D. thesis on Dutch-American relations. The Dutch, who are realists above all, know the boy's feat is hydraulically impossible, and therefore unworthy of local consumption; Dutch school children have never heard the story. Dutch realism is also so innate that not many years ago a statue was erected honoring the boy with his finger in the dike. It stands at Spaarndam, a small town near Haarlem, and it is a regular stop on guided tours, especially those taken by Americans. Dutchmen ignore it.

Belgian and Luxembourg tourist officials are as talented as the Dutch in devising ways of keeping a foreigner in a spending mood for an extra day or two. For centuries, local festivals have been an indigenous part of the lives of both countries. Today many are simply tourist attractions. Some, however, remain deeply religious—the Procession of the Holy Blood in Bruges and the pilgrimages to the shrine of Our Lady of Luxembourg in Luxembourg City, for example. Others, like Mardi Gras at Binche or "the Giants' Marriage" at Ath, are uninhibited carnivals of drinking, eating and dancing in the streets.

HOWEVER much the relics of the past dominate the tourist's-eye view, residents of the Low Countries are constantly aware of the changes that have taken place since the end of World War II. Such changes are occurring all over Europe, of course, but they are particularly noticeable in the Low Countries because they are contained within such a small space. The triangle occupied by Holland, Belgium and Luxembourg in the northwestern corner of Europe covers only 25,657 square miles—an area slightly larger than that of West Virginia. Even Switzerland, considered by many Americans the smallest nation outside the comic-opera class, is larger than either Holland or Belgium and 16 times the size of Luxembourg, whose area is officially listed at a precise 999 square miles. The greatest distance within the three countries—from the Frisian Islands in the North Sea to Belgium's border with France in the south—is only 270 miles; from Ostend on Belgium's west coast to Luxembourg's border with Germany in the east is only 180 miles. Close to 21 million people are squeezed within the Low Countries' borders—and squeezed is the only word. Holland alone has nearly 12 million people, 911 per square mile. It is the most densely populated country in the world.

PERHAPS because they stand out so strongly in the crowded streets of Amsterdam and Brussels, Delft and Bruges, Rotterdam and Antwerp, Utrecht and Luxembourg City, the old and the new in the Low Countries seem to jostle each other. Not far from Amsterdam's brand-new Hilton Hotel on any reasonably pleasant day—which by Dutch climatic standards means anything short of a downpour—is stationed one of the city's 15 *draaiorgels*, or barrel organs, huge, elaborately decorated affairs on wheels, all but extinct in the rest of the world. The other 14 are making their own oases elsewhere in the city, and 60 more are doing duty in the rest of the country. Their music brings harassed businessmen and women shoppers to a smiling halt. Belgians love music, too, but prefer that of their own making to what comes out of a machine; there are some 850 choral societies and more than 3,000 brass bands in the country and, depending on the carnival one attends, they all sometimes seem to be practicing ensemble. Nor are Luxembourgers far behind in music alfresco. "One

Luxembourger," runs a local saying, "a rose garden; two Luxembourgers, a kaffee-klatsch; three Luxembourgers, a band."

The Dutch and the Belgians are blessed with many good restaurants and a few excellent ones, and the food served at homes, while rarely *haute cuisine*, is substantial; but the prospect of dinner, whether in public or at home, does not stay Dutch or Belgians from pausing for a snack in the streets. In Belgium this treat is usually a paper cone of French fried potatoes —the Belgians (not the French) invented them and call them *patates frites* —bought at a corner stand, from which emanates the pervasive national odor: hot vegetable oil, stronger than the exhaust fumes of cars and motor scooters. The Dutch avoid potatoes in public, perhaps because they get so many at home; some shops which specialize in potatoes offer upward of a dozen varieties, giving Dutchmen who go in for that sort of thing a choice denied most other people. Street-eating for the Dutch is almost exclusively limited to the herring, although here and there opportunities for consuming smoked eel are found.

Mobile herring stands do a thriving business. In May and June, especially, when the new season's catch is brought in, they are as ubiquitous as ice cream vendors in American suburbs. Dutchmen leaving the Amsterdam stock exchange, one of the world's oldest, or entering the Rotterdam soccer stadium, the country's most modern, invariably stop at a herring stand, grasp the raw, cleaned fish by the tail, perhaps dip it in a bowl of chopped onions, tilt back their heads and munch until they reach the end. As with peanuts, one herring is never enough; the gourmet almost always gives a repeat performance.

ORIGIN OF A FAMILIAR NAME

Since the 16th Century, the official name of the Dutch homeland has been the Netherlands, although Dutchmen have given up trying to bring this to the attention of foreigners, who persist in calling the country Holland. The use of the term is, however, widely accepted. For centuries practically everyone who arrived on foreign shores from the Netherlands area was a "Hollander"—a native of the province of Holland. This province was the center of the nation's wealth and home to the captains and the adventurers who won an empire for the Dutch in the 17th Century. To this day Holland remains the Netherlands' most important region. Although it constitutes only about 16 per cent of the country's land area, it supports more than 40 per cent of the population.

Nourished, momentarily at least, by his potatoes or his herring, the Belgian or Dutchman continues with his chore of the moment— which, in his world abounding with anachronisms, may involve a decision on the shoring-up of a medieval church, the programing of a high-powered computer or the lowering of international tariffs. Contradictions pop up everywhere—in matters as local as a school board election or as universal as sex. In Holland, where a Calvinistic tradition dominates the moral attitude, men invariably precede women up a staircase, for a man may be led into temptation by the advantageous view of female legs and thighs. On Catholic-controlled beaches, the sexes are not only separated in the water, but on it as well; mixed boating is prohibited. At the same time, the center of Amsterdam contains one of the most wide-open, flourishing red-light districts in Western Europe.

In Belgium and Luxembourg, where Roman Catholicism is the predominant organized religion, children are raised in as strait-laced a fashion as were the offspring of the most devout New England Puritans. Yet a cabdriver in any Belgian town of reasonable size knows which hotels rent rooms by the hour, and the B-girls in Brussels and Luxembourg City enjoy full employment. In Belgium, too, the sale of hard liquor in cafés, bars and restaurants is illegal, but it is easier to buy a drink in most large Belgian cities today than it was in New York at the height of the speak-easy era. Bars call themselves clubs, and are remarkably open-minded about qualifications for membership.

Contradictions like these at least have the merit of being in the open where they can be considered amusing, embarrassing, irritating or

RELIGIOUS DIVISIONS in the Low Countries are indicated above. Each classification is meant only in a general sense; in each area there are people of every faith, plus nonbelievers.

property. But today tolerance suffers at home as Dutch Protestants and Catholics strive for political and social supremacy.

Protestants, who have dominated Dutch life for so much of the country's national history, resent the continual growth and increasing political power of the Catholics. The Catholic party is now the largest single political group in the country. In the postwar coalition governments Catholics usually have held the Ministry of Education. Some Protestants see this as a dangerous precedent. In 1963 the Catholics were still a minority with 38.3 per cent of the population to the Protestants' 38.8 per cent (3.9 per cent were members of other faiths and 19 per cent were nondenominational). Nearly all of the Catholics, however, vote as a bloc, a fact which enables them to collect what Protestants and freethinkers consider something more than their political due.

THE result of this religious feud is the *verzuiling* of Dutch society; the word comes from *zuil*, the Dutch word for column, and can be translated as "columnization." In Holland *verzuiling* characterizes a way of life which keeps Catholics from reading any but Catholic newspapers, listening to any but Catholic radio stations and joining any but Catholic clubs. It enjoins Protestants from reading any but Protestant newspapers, listening to any but the Protestant radio station and joining any but Protestant clubs. Nonchurch members deplore the existence of *verzuiling,* but they also have their own newspapers, radio stations and clubs. The result, of course, is that all sources of information tend to confirm preconceived views.

The staffing of a hospital and the design of a municipal building are often determined not by the skills of doctors or architects but by religious affiliation. *Verzuiling* is often so rigid that Catholic housewives seek out Catholic butchers, bakers, shoemakers and even cleaning women, while Protestant women tend to do business with Protestants. Some knowledgeable Dutchmen think that *verzuiling* is slowly breaking down among the youth of Holland,

reprehensible, depending on the point of view. More serious, though, as far as many thoughtful Dutch and Belgians are concerned, are schisms which are often invisible to the tourist's eye. Take religion in the Netherlands. The Dutch tradition of religious tolerance is as old as the country itself. The Netherlands' revolt against Spanish control in the 16th and 17th Centuries started because of the excesses of the Inquisition. Before independence was won, the country was welcoming Jews from Portugal and Spain and Huguenots from France, and had even promised religious freedom to the Catholics who chose to remain under its administration. It granted a haven to the Pilgrims when they felt compelled to depart England, and later it became one of the first nations in Europe to grant Jews the right to vote and to own and that it is also yielding under the pressure of a housing shortage that willy-nilly forces Catholics and Protestants to live on the same streets and even in the same apartment buildings. This may be so, but it is significant that boy scouts and girl scouts are still compartmented into Catholic and Protestant troops and that, except in a few intellectually oriented clubs, young people tend to separate themselves the way their elders do.

THE dichotomy in Belgium is different, but it is even sharper than in Holland. The internal split is so bitter, in fact, that civil war remains a constant threat. Ostensibly, the division derives from the lack of a national language. The Flemish Belgians of the North speak Dutch, and the Walloon Belgians of the South speak French. The schism—euphemistically referred to as "the linguistic question"—involves other Belgian splits as well. It is complicated by religious feelings; the Flemings are strongly bound by the Catholic Church. Among the Walloons, there are militant anticlerical feelings.

The split has historic origins. Since Roman times linguistic and cultural differences have persisted in the area. Ever since Belgium won its independence from Holland in 1830, French has been the country's dominant language. The Flemish movement for equal rights started with the coming of independence and has won some notable victories. There is no denying that the present situation is a vast improvement over the days when the Dutch-speaking Flemings were tried in courts conducted solely in French. In 1873, after two innocent Flemings were guillotined following a trial in which they did not understand a word, Dutch was introduced in Flemish courts, and interpreters were made available in both Flemish and Walloon courts. Not long after that, laws, official decrees, money and postage stamps were printed in both Dutch and French.

Officially, the kingdom of Belgium is both *Royaume de Belgique* and *Koninkrijk België,* but the more violent Flemings believe they are still a long way from completely equal rights.

LINGUISTIC DIVISIONS are shown on this map. The line roughly bisecting Belgium is a governmental one drawn for administrative purposes. Elsewhere the demarcations are unofficial.

The Flemings comprise 55 per cent of the Belgian population, yet they show all the characteristics of a minority. They claim—with some justification—that the top jobs in government, the armed forces and the foreign service go to the Walloons, and that French is still considered superior in Brussels, which by law is administered bilingually. It is true that Brussels street signs and subtitles on foreign movies give the two languages equal billing, but help-wanted ads for managerial positions appear in the French language newspapers and those for laborers appear in the Dutch language papers. Aside from what this says about comparative status, the Flemish complain the laborers are supervised by men whom they cannot understand. About 15 per cent of the Belgians speak both Dutch and French, but of course few of these persons are from the working classes.

In 1962, the Belgian parliament established a border which divided the country into its linguistic parts for administrative purposes. But extremist Flemings and Walloons are not satisfied with this. They would like to see a Belgian federation consisting of the states of Wallonia, Flanders and Brussels. Until that day comes, or some other solution is found, it seems likely that the two sides will continue to harass each other and, as in the world's cold war, come to actual blows from time to time.

THE Flemings take offense at seemingly innocent intrusions of the French language in their bailiwick. A few years ago in Antwerp, a city which is Flemish but which has a sizable French-speaking population, especially among the upper classes, a young Flemish tailor decided to open his own shop. He had taken the proper courses and was considered by the standards of his profession a fully accredited master tailor. Now the Dutch language does not have a word or phrase which fully connotes the loftiness of a master tailor as opposed to an ordinary tailor. French, on the other hand, has the precise coupling: *maître tailleur*. The young man put up his shingle with the two French words following his name. The next morning he discovered his shop window smashed.

At the Museum of Fine Arts in the Flemish city of Ghent, which courteously follows the rules of bilingualism as befits an institution devoted to art, small gold cards identify several paintings that were donated by a group called Friends of the Museum—*Les Amis du Musée* and *De Vrienden van het Museum*. Not long ago one of the militant Flemings—they are called Flamingants by the Walloons—took a sharp instrument to each of these signs and crudely scratched out the French phrase.

Yet these manifestations of the Belgian strife are sweet reasonableness compared to the outbreak on October 14, 1962, when an estimated 50,000 Flemings marched in Brussels to dramatize their demands. Their placards read "The language wall is a money wall," "The language

of the workers must be the language of the factory" and "Flemish doctors for Flemish sick." No Belgian flags were displayed; instead, many marchers carried the flag of Flanders or the Dutch flag. (Some Flemings seek secession from Belgium and annexation to Holland, but this is not considered a serious possibility; Belgian ties are too strong, and Dutch Protestants are not likely to approve the sudden acquisition of four million Catholics.)

The demonstration soon turned into a riot. Heckling by Walloon spectators and rejoinders by Flemish marchers gave way to clubs, fists, barrel staves, eggs, firecrackers, gasoline bombs and beer bottles. Before 4,000 gendarmes aided by riot squads broke up the battle, downtown Brussels was littered with debris and 19 Belgians were injured. Some 40 persons were arrested, and after the streets were cleared around midnight, the remains of trampled baby chicks were found outside the stock exchange where the roughest fighting took place. The chick was being used by the Flemings as a grim joke on their relationship to the Walloons, whose symbol is the rooster. The joke was perhaps less ironic than the slogan that is inscribed twice on the Belgian coat of arms: *L'union fait la force* and *Eendracht maakt macht,* which in both languages means "Union makes strength."

THE existence of conflict and contradiction militates against generalizations about the Low Countries. Generalizations abound, of course, and at their simplest level some may even have merit. The Dutch and Belgians are neat and clean: this has been part of the canon since the 17th Century, when foreign visitors were first impressed with the mania for cleanliness in these countries. Sir William Temple, a British ambassador to the Netherlands in the late 17th Century, found when dining in a private home that "every time I spit, a tight handsome wench (that stood in the room with a clean cloth in her hand) was presently down to wipe it up, and rub the board clean."

The same spirit moves modern Dutch and Belgian housewives to the famous habit of taking brush, soap and water once a week to the steps and sidewalks in front of their homes. In Holland and Flemish Belgium this chore is performed on Saturday, which is called *schoonmaakdag*, "clean-making day"; in the French-speaking part of Belgium it is called *faire son vendredi*, "do one's Friday"—although the task is often left for Saturday, too. John L. Brown, an American Foreign Service officer who was stationed in Brussels for many years, recalled recently that he once "attempted to dissuade our maid from going out in a snow flurry to wash the sidewalk, but she firmly rejected my improper suggestion. She realized, as I did not, that our standing as a family, as well as her personal honor, was at stake."

BUT if Holland and Belgium can be linked by a common devotion to cleanliness, they are divided in their attitude toward neatness. The Dutch rate the quality of *netjes* very highly. In the flexible way of the language, the word combines neatness with orderliness and implies a handsome appearance as well. It is definitely a compliment when applied to a home or apartment, a girl's dress, the look of an entire town (after its fish markets have been scrubbed down), and to the way a government clerk keeps his files. So addicted is the Dutchman to *netjes* that when Holland was invaded in World War II, the Nazis found perfectly maintained and up-to-date records of Dutch identity cards, a bonanza for the occupation forces. It became one of the prime jobs of the Dutch resistance to systematically raid town halls and destroy or jumble files. The Belgians, on the other hand, are a less orderly people; their files were in such a bad state—lost, misplaced or faultily filled out—that the Germans could make almost no use of them.

Since the two countries take opposite positions on the way records are kept it should not come as a surprise that they have even more serious differences. There is indeed a long tradition of antipathy. The Dutch have never quite forgiven the Belgians for remaining loyal to Spain during the Dutch war for independence more than 300 years ago, and Belgians still rankle when reminded that for a brief unhappy period in the 19th Century they were actually part of the Kingdom of the Netherlands. Belgians resented Dutch neutrality during World War I, when Belgium was invaded and brutally treated by the Germans; the Dutch envied Belgium's relatively quick recovery from World War II, while they had to live with price and wage controls and rationing well into the post-war period.

If a foreigner's logic shows that the Low Countries should long ago have split along historic linguistic and religious lines, the Dutch, the Belgians and the Luxembourgers argue that despite inner tension unity is their primary strength. Given their size and their lack of natural borders, they are as easy to invade now as they were when Julius Caesar's legions conquered them in the First Century B.C. Their security, they realized after Hitler's Panzers overran them in the 20th Century A.D., lies within the framework of a larger alliance. They were among the first nations to embrace the North Atlantic Treaty Organization, and long before the birth of the Common Market, of which they are forceful members, they had formed an economic union called Benelux (an acronym formed from Belgium, Netherlands and Luxembourg). Neither Belgium nor Holland has been happy with some of the decisions affecting them made by the United Nations, but there is no significant feeling in either country that they should withdraw.

THE Low Countries occupy one of the most strategic and wealthy land areas in Europe. (Minuscule Luxembourg, for example, blessed with rich iron ore deposits, is Western Europe's sixth largest steel producer.) As a result, the three nations, separately and together, have had an importance in the world vastly disproportionate to their size. While it is probably no longer true, as a 13th Century historian wrote, that "he who holds Flanders holds the North Sea," the position of the Low Countries, between Europe's heartland and the open sea, is still a major factor in the movement of European goods to market. The Rhine, Meuse and Scheldt, the great waterways from Germany, Switzerland and northern France, still carry seemingly endless convoys of loaded barges to the ports of Rotterdam and Antwerp. Indeed, the traffic is so heavy that Rotterdam is second only to New York among the world's ports and, given the present rate of growth of each, will within 10 years be first in both tonnage and value of goods handled.

Geographically, there are only slight differences among the three countries. Holland's topography is almost completely unbroken—as flat as it appears in the landscapes created by its master painters. Only in a few sections can hills be found, and these would not be noteworthy anywhere except in Holland; several moors in the east give the impression of a rolling terrain, although few rise as high as 300 feet. What pass for Dutch mountains can be found only in the southeast, where some hills are as high as 1,000 feet. But it is the low-lying flatness which impresses, whether at Schiphol Airport, near Amsterdam, which announces its sea level as minus 13 feet, or in the meeting of land and sky at what seems to be a right angle off in the distance.

HOLLAND's flatness carries into Belgium across the Flemish plains, but indications of a gentle rise are already visible. The central part of Belgium is on a higher plateau, and the southern part higher still, beginning at about 600 feet on the right bank of the Meuse and rising to 2,100 feet. There, toward the border with Luxembourg, is the wooded Ardennes plateau on which the Battle of the Bulge—the Nazis' last counteroffensive in World War II—took place. Luxembourg is part of the plateau, although the southern part of the country, including the capital city of Luxembourg, breaks up into deep valleys and craggy hills.

There is more change in the physical characteristics of the people, moving from north to south, than there is in the landscape. Distinctive regional types appear. The Dutch of the northern provinces are fair and blue-eyed. Darker types predominate farther south, and most Dutchmen would look at home in Brussels. In the Walloon provinces and in Luxembourg increasingly darker features, like those of the French, are seen. Both men and women throughout the Low Countries have a rugged handsomeness; few women are truly beautiful, but most have healthy good looks.

SUPERFICIALLY, at least in Holland and northern Belgium, there is a personality resemblance to the German because of a character trait known as *eigenwijs,* or know-it-all. It is applied to the superciliousness with which Dutch and Belgians declare their views about the United States or the business ability of their next-door neighbor. But it never reaches arrogance, mostly because it is saved by a sense of humor and some humility; when a Dutchman says, "That is typically Dutch," he is not bragging, but is usually talking about a shortcoming which he considers indigenous.

There is no scale on which to balance the geography which unifies the Low Countries against the history which sets them apart, but at present, and for the foreseeable future, Holland, Belgium and Luxembourg are committed to a policy of unity, not alone for themselves but for all of Western Europe. It hardly matters whether this has occurred despite their many differences or because of factors which bind their lands and people. It may be some of both. Nor should this seem especially strange to Americans since, except for the disparity in size, much the same basis for union exists in the Low Countries as in the United States. F. Gunther Eyck, a historian with the American University in Washington, D.C., concluded in a recent study on Holland, Belgium and Luxembourg that a practical and lasting unity is probable. He explains the discrepancy of inner tension and outward harmony among the Low Countries in words which might just as well apply to the United States: "Their people look for union through diversity rather than oneness through uniformity."

A woman strides across a stone-paved bridge spanning one of the many canals that have made Ghent a flourishing inland port.

A Driving Energy Creating Order and Precision

The familiar stereotype of the Low Countries includes neat fields, scrubbed towns and an atmosphere of sturdy energy. For once, the stereotype is accurate. The farms are meticulously cultivated; calm rivers and canals flow between carefully tended banks. But it is particularly in the towns and cities that a special neatness and order, strength and solidity make themselves apparent. The streets are clean and the houses seem rooted, indestructible. More important, even the most densely populated areas seldom appear overcrowded. It is as if everything had its place and every person had his settled round. The Low Countries, even though internally divided by rivalries and jealousies—and driving energetically to improve their position as modern industrial nations—preserve an order established by generations of forebears.

HANDSOME GUILDHALLS look down on the Lys River from the Quai aux Herbes in Ghent. The wide, squat building third from the left is the city's ancient granary, built around 1200. Second from left is the masons' guildhall. To the far side of the granary are the tiny customhouse and then the tall, imposing halls built by the Grain Measurers and the Free Boatmen.

BRONZE STATUE in the Grand' Place of Bruges, a square in the heart of the city, honors the leaders of a 1302 revolt of Flemish workers who rose up against the city's patrician rulers.

SYMMETRICAL FAÇADE of a house in Rijswijk, Holland, is mirrored in the placid waters of a wide canal as a brightly clad boy pedals by. Rijswijk is a growing suburb of The Hague.

ROLLING FIELDS border the small town of Echternach in an agricultural area of Luxembourg. The pointed spires belong to a Benedictine abbey and church founded around the year 700.

QUIET VALLEY has its peace disturbed *(right)* as a freight train crosses the viaduct connecting Luxembourg City with its suburb of Pfaffenthal. Luxembourg is rich in iron deposits.

neighbors and more heavily industrialized, retains its own variety of parklike neatness

CARRYING A SHRINE, celebrators of Tournai, Belgium *(opposite),* join in an annual festival which commemorates the city's miraculous deliverance from the plague in the year 1092.

CHATTING IN GROUPS, students gather on the paths of a carefully tended park in Brussels waiting for a nearby library to open. The building at right houses Common Market offices.

The fortress of Bouillon looms grimly above Belgium's placid Semois River. Its foundations date from the 11th Century when it was the

stronghold of Godfrey of Bouillon, a hero of the First Crusade.

2

Years
of Turbulence
and Revolt

THE precedent for treating the Low Countries as a unit goes back to the *Commentaries on the Gallic Wars* written by Julius Caesar, who used the name Gallia Belgica to identify roughly the area now occupied by Holland, Belgium and Luxembourg. But even then, as Caesar knew, there were distinct tribal differences in this strange corner of the empire. This mixed bag of peoples whom he called the Belgae—among them Celts in Flanders, Germanic tribes (including the Batavi and the Frisians) in the north and east, and Gauls in the south—was not easy to handle even under military pressure. Caesar conquered the tribes, but the job required seven campaigns which left him with a reluctant admiration for their fighting skill. "Of all these peoples," he reported to Rome, "the Belgae are the most courageous." The conquest brought the area the benefits of Roman civilization: a common official language, law, order and roads. But the tribal differences within the area prevented political unification. It is quite clear, even from the scanty knowledge we have of the early history of the Low Countries, that if the unity they have established in recent years is real it is despite tradition, not because of it.

However unity fared, durable Low Countries traditions were born under the Roman reign, including a love of freedom and a willingness to fight for it. Revolts kept the Roman troops busy. None was successful, but one at least provided heroes who have endured for 1,900 years, thanks to the writings of Tacitus, the Roman historian. Tacitus was impressed by the rebellion in 69 A.D. of the Batavi, who lived on what is now Dutch soil under the leadership of Civilis, a member of the tribe who had become an officer in the Roman army. Despite initial victories, the Batavi were no match for Roman legions. In a brief but turbulent encounter the Batavi were suppressed.

The revolt in the face of large odds impressed later generations as much as it did Tacitus. In the 17th Century, following the Dutch revolt against Spain, Hugo Grotius, Holland's great authority on international law, cited the Batavi as Holland's first freedom fighters, a view which gained wide popularity. From his day to this, Dutch school children have been brought up on the story of the Batavi.

ASIDE from immortality, the Batavi achieved nothing with their revolt. It was, however, a hint of future troubles for the Romans, for in time their overextended empire began to deteriorate. By the Third Century A.D., the Germanic tribes were starting to overrun Roman outposts. But as Roman control weakened, fresh invaders entered the Low Countries. Angles and Saxons conquered the Frisians and established a joint kingdom. The Franks moved into the southern region. They converted many of the natives to Christianity, but it took them several centuries to conquer and largely Christianize the Frisian-Anglo-Saxon kingdom. Not until 776 were the Frisians subdued. Despite the conquest, the Frisians maintained their identity, and even to this day the

Frisian language remains distinct from Dutch.

From the Sixth Century through the Eighth, the Frankish kings sought to impose unity on the Low Countries, but had little more success than the Romans. With the death of Charlemagne in 814, Frankish rule disintegrated. At this juncture, a double invasion—Vikings from the North and a devastating series of floods—left the Low Countries almost completely in ruins. Charlemagne's quarreling heirs divided control of the area among themselves. Their lax overlordship, however, permitted the growth of local principalities in the 10th and 11th Centuries. The region was carved into feudal domains whose names survive today as those of Dutch and Belgian provinces: Flanders, Brabant, Hainaut, Limburg, Namur, Holland, Gelderland, Zeeland and Friesland.

THE rulers of these principalities switched their allegiances often, allying or subordinating themselves by turns to the kings of France, the emperors of Germany or the kings of England. The counts of Flanders, beginning with the reign of Baudouin with the Beautiful Beard (988-1035), increased their power through wise marriages and skillful administration and proudly proclaimed themselves "First after God." The counts and countesses of Luxembourg found safety and prosperity in a city built around the hilltop fortification that the Franks had called Lucilinburhuc (the small fort). At Liège and Utrecht, bishoprics flourished.

With the growth of trade and movement in the Middle Ages, mercantile towns developed which were to have an enormous influence on the history and national character of the Low Countries. In the closely knit communities the new middle (or burgher) class began to display local pride and a tough realism, and to make its first strivings toward self-government and independence. As the French observer, Alexis de Tocqueville, was to write centuries later, the early towns were for the Belgians "the primary school of liberty." Around the dams built in Holland in the 12th and 13th Centuries, cities grew. Traveling merchants set up shops, and an increasing number of people was drawn to the new towns. By the end of the 12th Century more than 40 municipalities existed in Flanders. Ghent, Bruges and Ypres had more than 50,000 people each, supported by the great wool and linen trade.

Not everyone was pleased by the growth of towns, a merchant class and the new freedom. Churchmen especially saw new dangers in the breakdown of the old class structure. As early as the 11th Century, a monk from Brabant looked with disfavor upon some merchants of Tiel, one of the newfangled cities. "Refractory, undisciplined men," he called them, "who administer justice not according to law but to suit themselves. They claim that the emperor has allowed them to do so in writing. They forswear themselves daily, see no crime in adultery, drink heavily, and hail with roars of laughter that man as the most popular among them who, in the foulest language, incites them to guzzle wine."

This may have been an accurate appraisal, but the monk's criticism was certainly a minority view. The rights and privileges the merchants received "in writing" had been won slowly and with great effort, and were important landmarks on the road to human freedom. The most important of the municipal charters is known as the Joyeuse Entrée (Joyous Entry). Issued in 1356, it comes close to being the Magna Carta of Belgium and Luxembourg. In it, the Duke and Duchess of Brabant promised that they would impose no restrictions, except legal taxes, on trade; pledged not to declare offensive war "except at the advice, will and consent of our good cities and lands"; and gave the subjects the right to revolt if the duke exceeded his legal powers.

THE merchants and the industrialists benefited most from the autonomy thus granted. In time they came to dominate the local society and, since trade and manufacture were of greater importance than agriculture, wide areas around the cities as well. The sense of security which this fostered led to the formation of new associations—town councils for political expression, guilds for professional purposes, universities for schooling promising youths. Pride of city or town was strong, and it has been durable; local patriotism is still a major characteristic of the Low Countries.

By the middle of the 14th Century two Low Countries provinces had started to move ahead of their neighbors. Holland and Zeeland on the coast discovered the profits to be found in the Baltic trade. Shipbuilding and sea travel increased rapidly, not only founding the great Dutch maritime tradition, but laying the basis for the region's future naval strength. At about the same time, another gift from the sea all but guaranteed steadily increasing prosperity: in 1384 Willem Beukels of Zeeland found that fresh herring would keep for long periods if gutted and stored in barrels with alternate layers of salt. When 30 years later a fisherman from the city of Hoorn devised a successful large net, the Dutch herring fleets grew to enormous sizes to meet the insatiable European demand for the fish.

ALTHOUGH by the end of the 14th Century there was some degree of interdependence among the provinces and cities of the Low Countries, there was no unifying force within the region. When unity did come it was imposed by outsiders—first by the dukes of Burgundy, who assembled an empire with a recipe mixing intrigue, inheritance, warfare, marriage and luck, and then by the equally astute Hapsburgs. By the 16th Century the Hapsburgs had established a domain which included most of central Europe, Spain and its colonies, parts of Italy and much of the Low Countries. The most renowned of the Hapsburgs, Charles V, was born in Ghent in 1500. To rule the northwestern section of his empire, he established a central government for the Low Countries, set up a council of state largely made up of noblemen and assigned a *stadhouder*, or governor, to each of the provinces.

Native son though he was, Charles spent very little time in the Low Countries; duties elsewhere in his empire were too pressing, and for all practical purposes his aunt, Margaret of Austria, ruled the provinces until her death in 1530. She and her successor, Charles' half sister Mary of Hungary, governed intelligently, and prosperity increased. Annual and biennial fairs attracted many foreigners who were amazed at some of the customs. In 1506 an Italian visitor wrote that Antwerp's women "have very free manners, and spend all their leisure in dancing, singing and making music."

FOR the southern provinces it was an extraordinarily creative period. For roughly 200 years Flemish and Walloon painters, architects, musicians and scholars were outstanding in Europe. The Van Eyck brothers, Hans Memling and Rogier van der Weyden did portraits of royalty and of rich merchants, and painted Biblical scenes which are as alive today as when they were first executed. Churches, town halls and guildhalls, many of which still stand in Belgium, were erected in great numbers. The University of Louvain, which was founded in 1425, attracted students from all over Europe, and attained such status that its rector controlled a police force, a court of law and a prison. Gerhardus Mercator invented a method of portraying the earth's global surface on a flat map. Andreas Vesalius contributed to knowledge of the body with anatomical studies.

While the creative arts flourished, there were divisive influences at work which were to undermine the political unity which Charles V imposed on the Low Countries. During his reign came the rise and spread of Lutheranism and Calvinism. Charles, a devoted Catholic, was allied to Rome. In 1525, the Inquisition's first Low Countries victims were burned at the stake in Utrecht. By the time Charles abdicated in 1555 to spend the rest of his life in prayer and semiseclusion in a monastery, the Inquisition had become an instrument of public policy. Charles bequeathed the Low Countries (among other possessions) to his son, Philip II. The legacy led Philip to a career—unsuccessful, as it eventually was to turn out—of barring

Protestantism from his extensive territories.

Philip's rule was harsh. He was a meticulous administrator, knowledgeable about detail but shortsighted in decision. He would not learn Dutch, which kept him from most of the common people, nor speak French, which kept him from both people and nobles. To strengthen his position against the new heresies, he gradually reduced the rights which had been slowly accruing to his Low Countries subjects over the years. Local self-government became a fiction, taxes were increased to pay for foreign wars, and religious persecution was stepped up. Protests by the people and the nobility were useless; Philip stayed in Spain while his half sister, Margaret of Parma, ruled as his regent with good intentions but no real authority.

In the meantime, Protestantism was sweeping through the southern provinces and was moving north. Soon the most highly organized opposition to Philip was centered among the Calvinists, whose leaders in Geneva had told them that they had a right to revolt when the Church of God or its people were persecuted. The people of the Low Countries were ready for revolt; all they lacked was strong leadership. When that came the Low Countries were prepared to embark on their most important national adventure.

THE Eighty Years' War began with a peaceful but dramatic gesture of protest. When it ended the Netherlands was strong and independent and Spain's power was all but broken. The protest came on April 5, 1566, when hundreds of Low Countries nobles marched through the streets of Brussels to the home of Margaret of Parma to protest religious persecution. Many of the noblemen carried the beggar's bowl and pouch which once had signified that their devotion to the king would hold until they were reduced to beggars. That, and the taunt by the regime's backers that they had put themselves outside "good society," gave them the name of "beggars" (*gueux* in French, *geuzen* in Dutch). As other rebels have done, the nobles and their followers turned the term of derision into a battle cry, and the "Songs of the Beggars" spread through the Low Countries.

More important than a song or a name, the protest of the nobles produced a leader, William of Orange, called "the Silent" because of his skill at hiding his thoughts under a flow of pleasant talk. William gave the revolt its goals: independence and religious tolerance.

WILLIAM was as shocked by Protestant excesses as he was by Catholic intolerance. He had nothing to do with an outbreak of iconoclasm in the summer of 1566 during which Catholic churches throughout the Low Countries were broken into and their sacred images smashed. But after Margaret's troops had restored order, he was among the thousands of Calvinists and non-Calvinists who exiled themselves in order to escape execution. Margaret's victory was, however, not enough for Philip. He sent Fernando Alvarez de Toledo, Duke of Alba, on a punitive expedition to the Low Countries. Alba soon displaced Margaret as ruler and organized the Bloody Council, a special court for treason cases, which in a short time condemned more than 8,000 people to death. Alba's purpose was to break the aristocratic leadership of the "Beggars Revolt," and in this he succeeded, with one notable exception. William the Silent, in exile, had plans to return.

At first, William waged war against Alba with armies raised in Germany and France. But the land forces were hardly more than a minor annoyance to Alba, and William turned to the "Sea Beggars"—exiles from the Low Countries who equipped and manned vessels to attack Spanish shipping. Soon the Sea Beggars started to liberate coastal towns from Spanish rule, and the idea of independence from Spain spread from the province of Holland to the interior. In November 1576, in a document called the Pacification of Ghent, representatives of all but one of the provinces of the Low Countries pledged to work together for victory over Spain. (Royalist Luxembourg was the one which did not sign the pact, an indication that it would retain its separate status in the future.)

Less than a year after this show of strength William made a triumphant entry into Brussels.

At this point, internal conflicts changed the nature of the rebellion—and the history of the Low Countries. A party called the "Malcontents" was formed by Catholic nobles who resented William's growing power and feared the new Calvinist strength. The Malcontents soon won followers in the Walloon area, and after 1578—when Philip had replaced Alba with the moderate Alessandro Farnese, Duke of Parma—in the provinces of Flanders and Brabant as well. In 1579, the southern provinces—roughly today's Belgium—started making peace treaties with Spain. The northern provinces not only issued a strong declaration of independence but also bound themselves by the Union of Utrecht to keep fighting. By 1584, when William was assassinated by a Catholic fanatic, what had started as a noblemen's protest had turned into the Dutch war for independence.

In 1609 Spain, weakened by war with England and France as well as the Netherlands, agreed to a cessation of hostilities. Although officially peace did not come until 1648, the truce tacitly recognized the independence of the Netherlands; for the Dutch it was a signal for the release of energies on a grand scale and in many directions—exploration, trade, art and science. In Holland's *Gouden Eeuw* (Golden Century) more than 1,000 ships were turned out every year. By 1650, the Dutch navy was twice the size of the English and French fleets put together. The ubiquitous Dutch vessels were in the Pacific, the Mediterranean, the Baltic and the Atlantic and along the African coast. Dutch explorers were finding new sea routes, new fishing grounds and new lands from the Arctic to Latin America.

WITH the fresh flow of wealth Amsterdam, the capital and major port of the country, grew rapidly, and fabulous town houses were built along the new canals. The new wealth inspired an upsurge in art. Painters flourished, and although Rembrandt van Rijn, Frans Hals (who emigrated from the Belgian provinces), Jan Vermeer, Jacob van Ruisdael and Jan Steen are best known, hundreds of others also caught the Dutch landscape and the Dutch people in town and country with talent and sensitivity.

NO nation, however wealthy, was likely to maintain so spectacular a level of achievement for long. By the following century, the Dutch themselves, surfeited with success, lost much of the boldness which had marked their rise. National purpose and leadership all but disappeared, and the Dutch, who had dominated the seas in the 17th Century—their war fleets had once sailed up the Thames—were an easy mark for England in the 18th. Internal dissension opened the way in 1795 for liberal Dutchmen, inspired by the French Revolution and aided by the French army, to take over the state and proclaim a Batavian Republic—named after the legendary Batavi.

The two centuries which encompassed Holland's rise and decline were years of turmoil and unrest for the southern provinces. Belgium became the playing field for Europe's war games. Louis XIV of France embarked on a great imperialist adventure in the 17th Century, and in the course of it Brussels was bombarded and some 3,800 homes were burned. Between 1702 and 1713 three decisive battles of the War of the Spanish Succession took place in Belgium. One of the decisions of the war was to place Belgium again under foreign rule, this time that of Austria. As if this were not bad enough, the Dutch kept the Scheldt estuary closed to Belgian trade, all but ruining Antwerp as a port. In 1789, revolution—spreading, like Holland's, from France—brought a republic into being, but the Austrians had no trouble regaining control. They in turn lost it almost at once to the French Republic, which simply incorporated Belgium into France.

When Napoleon became emperor he did nothing to change Belgium's status, but decided that Holland was a proper outlet for the talents of his brother Louis, then in need of employment. He abolished the Batavian Republic and established the Kingdom of Holland in 1806, installing Louis as king. Although he showed a regard for Dutch interests, Louis could not control his subjects; during the Napoleonic Wars enemy British goods were smuggled in and out of Dutch ports at will. In disgust at such loose management, Napoleon forced his brother to abdicate and made Holland part of the empire, too. When Napoleon's collapse came in 1815 at Waterloo—perhaps the only foreign battle on Belgian soil the natives have ever enjoyed—the Low Countries were on their own once more, although not to Belgium's satisfaction. The Congress of Vienna saw less need for an independent Belgium than for a strong dependable Netherlands which could serve as a buffer to France, and awarded the Belgian provinces to Holland.

THE forced integration of Holland and Belgium as the Kingdom of the Netherlands lasted only 15 years. On August 25, 1830, the Brussels Opera House was presenting Auber's *The Mute of Portici,* which celebrates the revolt of the Neapolitans against the French. To an audience composed of students and liberals who had been protesting Dutch discrimination toward Belgians, the parallel was clear. Demonstrations in the opera house moved to the streets. Word spread swiftly to the provinces; within a month street fighting was raging in Brussels, and the small Dutch army was unable to put down the insurrection. In September a provisional government was established, and by the end of the year European nations began to recognize Belgian independence. On June 4, 1831, a newly formed national congress elected a German prince, Leopold of Saxe-Coburg, King of the Belgians, and in 1839, a stubborn Holland signed a treaty which acknowledged the sovereignty of Belgium.

Given the turbulent history of the Low Countries, few people would have predicted that the new state of affairs would last. But the revolution that started in an opera house marked the real beginning of the modern Dutch and Belgian states.

The 16th Century cathedral in Ghent (background) seems dwarfed by the city's massive belfry (left foreground), completed in 1339.

A Legacy of Beauty Wrenched from Adversity

The small lands that make up the Low Countries are thickly sown with ruined forts and castles, reminders of the long, troubled centuries when the area was a battleground for the warring monarchs of Europe. But they also abound in great cathedrals, fine guildhalls and ancient universities—evidence of the peoples' unquenchable desire to create lasting monuments and a firm culture. Again and again, grandeur and beauty have risen from the ground.

MASSIVE CASTLE of Vianden tops a wooded hill overlooking the Our River Valley in the much-fought-over Ardennes forest of Luxembourg. Begun in the 12th Century, the castle was enlarged until its Knights' Hall could accommodate 500 men-at-arms. As evidence of a long history of strife, tiny Luxembourg is dotted with the remains of no less than 135 castles and forts.

POWDER STOREHOUSES, called the Three Acorns after their acorn-shaped roof decorations, are all that remain of Fort Thüngen, once part of the fortified ring around Luxembourg City.

RUINED WALLS of Brandenbourg Castle stand near Luxembourg's Blees River. A powerful family, the Brandenbourgs took their name from a part of Germany which they once ruled.

SOARING BULK of Notre-Dame-du-Sablon in Brussels *(opposite)* dwarfs a young cyclist. Completed in the 16th Century with money raised by a rich guild, the church is a fine example of late Gothic style.

CARVED MANTLE looms above two magistrates in a chamber of Bruges' Palace of Justice. In medieval times Bruges was a great trading and manufacturing city with a population larger than London's.

LECTURE IN FRENCH at Louvain inspires a largely feminine class to eager note-taking. Every course at Louvain is given in two languages, in French for Walloons, in Dutch for Flemings.

LECTURE IN DUTCH absorbs some of the 7,941 Flemish students at Louvain *(below)*. The process of duplicating the curriculum has put a noticeable strain on the university's resources.

BELGIUM'S LOUVAIN, *founded in 1425, remains one of the leading universities in Europe*

MODERN LIBRARY, which has a large, well-lit reading room, was built in the 1920s, largely with money raised in America, after its predecessor was burned by the Germans in 1914.

STUDENT CAFE called the Restaurant Alma *(left)* provides a social center for Louvain's 15,134 students. Many priests, like the robed cleric shown here, study for degrees at Louvain.

In a photograph taken about 1890 in Poerbolinggo, Java, a Dutch colonial official and his family, with several of their servants,

pose on the lawn before their pillared, tree-shaded residence.

3

The Toppled Empires

IN 1962, when the Dutch government formally gave up its claims to Netherlands New Guinea, an area larger than Japan, the event was heralded with appropriately large headlines, but it provided less conversational material in the cafés of The Hague, Amsterdam and Rotterdam than the start of the new soccer season. History-conscious though they are, the Dutch did not seem to care that an empire that had lasted more than 350 years had dwindled to a wedge of land on the South American coast and a few tiny islands in the Caribbean. The loss of Indonesia in 1949 had been exceedingly disturbing, but 13 years later the Dutch could regard the surrender of their last large colony as the anticlimax it really was.

Just two years earlier, in 1960, Belgium had granted independence to the Congo, which it had held only since 1908. The subsequent violence in the Congo has been attributed by some critics to the precipitate speed with which Belgium cut its colonial connections. But in

39

Belgium the decision to free the Congo, whatever the consequences, was generally accepted; some Belgians even welcomed the end of empire, and the 4 per cent drop in national income that resulted from the loss of the Congo was considered a bargain price.

THE acquisition, exploitation—and dissolution—of tremendous colonial possessions in Asia and Africa are important aspects of the history of the Low Countries, and keys to understanding the character of the Dutch and Belgians. Dutch imperialism goes back, naturally enough, to the country's golden century. In 1596, even before independence had been won from Spain, four Dutch ships had sailed to Java. Two years later, 22 ships sailed for the Far East; 13 returned loaded with exotic spices. The profits from this expedition were large enough to inspire other shippers to follow. Within a few years the competition among traders was so intense that prices rose too high to assure the continuation of profits; native chiefs became rich, but the Dutch entrepreneurs barely covered their expenses.

Dutch realism was rarely so explicitly expressed as in the solution to this problem: end competition, and make the East Indian trade a monopoly. This seemed such a logical and altogether desirable answer that when the United East India Company was formed in 1602 with a government-approved monopoly of all trade and shipping outside Atlantic Ocean areas, six and a half million guilders was raised in very little time.

Although the charter granted the East India Company full power to exercise all rights of sovereignty, it did not actually call for colonization; company ships were empowered to wage war against Spanish and Portuguese ships, and were even given a state subsidy to defray expenses for weapons, but the main purpose was trade. Within 10 years East India Company ships were doing business in Japan, China, Indochina, Siam, India, Arabia and Australia.

Because of the military subsidy it is hard to tell how much money the company actually made, but only eight years after its establishment it distributed a dividend of 162 per cent on the original investment. The figure might have been greater except that there was a shortage of the kinds of trade goods the natives wanted, and the Dutch had to pay in gold and silver. When the solution to this costly method of acquiring spices, silk and chinaware was found, the Dutch were on their way to great prosperity—and an empire.

The solution was devised by the governor-general of the Indies, Jan Pieterszoon Coen, who arranged an intra-Asian trading system whereby Dutch ships carried goods from one country to another. The profits from this carrying trade thereupon were used to buy the merchandise which was shipped to Europe. Coen founded the city of Batavia—later to become the capital of the Dutch East Indies and, renamed Djakarta, the capital of Indonesia—as the center for his Asiatic trade; and despite occasional battles with the Spanish, Portuguese and English, the city and the East India Company prospered.

ONCE, the English narrowly missed beating the Dutch in a naval battle off Batavia. The close call turned Coen vindictive, and shortly afterward he was further embittered when the Netherlands government at home concluded an agreement to cooperate with the British in Asia. In 1623 Coen had eight Englishmen executed for an alleged plot to seize the Dutch fortress at Amboina. The English reacted bitterly to what they called the "Amboina massacre" and used it as a rallying cry in their three wars against the Dutch in the 17th Century. In his fury, James I of England dispensed with diplomatic language; he bluntly told the Dutch ambassador in London that "you have a man in the Indies who deserves to be hanged."

Coen was not hanged, and may never have heard the complaint; he was too busy establishing an empire. In the second half of the 17th Century, the Dutch moved from cargo carrying and trading to political control. Before the century was out they were finding agricultural riches in the soil, and by the early 1700s they had struck the richest lode of all—coffee. Throughout the 18th Century coffee was the chief export of the Indies, and it remained so even after sugar and indigo were found profitable.

All this time the colonies were still, strictly speaking, under the control of the East India Company, not the Dutch government. During the fourth Anglo-Dutch war (1780-1784), however, shipping to Europe became impossible, and the company found itself in financial trouble. By the time there seemed to be a chance to save it, Holland possessed a new government, the Batavian Republic inspired by the French Revolution. Prince William of Orange (then hereditary *stadhouder*, or governor), who had fled to England, requested the colonial governors to cooperate with the British navy until he returned to office. But the governors continued to take orders from the new Batavian government, which gradually increased its control over colonial policy. After that it was only a matter of formalities, and in 1798 the Dutch government officially took over the possessions and debts of the East India Company.

EMPIRE BUILDER Jan Pieterszoon Coen (1587-1630) was instrumental in establishing Dutch control over the rich East Indies.

The Dutch colonies were harshly ruled in the 19th Century. Government officials pushed for high production of coffee and sugar, no matter what the cost in human lives. Few persons in Holland were aware of the exploitation that was the source of the swelling profits. By mid-century, however, the Liberal party had added Indonesian reform to its platform and demanded that slavery be abolished. Not long after this was done in 1860, the Dutch were aroused by the publication of *Max Havelaar*, a novel by Eduard Douwes Dekker, who wrote under the pen name Multatuli (He Who Has Suffered Much). The book searingly criticized the colonial system. Dekker was a former colonial official who had resigned in protest against the system. His cause soon gained enough adherents to force the introduction of reforms.

With the wealth of the Indies as a bulwark, the Netherlands moved slowly, peacefully, almost smugly, through the years between the loss of the Belgian provinces in 1830 (see Chapter 2) and World War II. Actually, Holland did not accept Belgium's new status as an independent nation until 1839. The nine-year delay was largely due to the stubbornness of William I, who had been named to the Dutch throne created in 1814 by an assembly of leading citizens after his father, Prince William, had died in English exile. The Dutch people themselves were relieved, since the end of the bickering with Belgium meant they could devote themselves to domestic problems which had been neglected for years.

Reforms—including a liberal constitution—were pushed which started the Netherlands on the road to democracy. When ministerial responsibility was introduced in 1840, William I abdicated in favor of his son, William II. Under him the country's democratic base was broadened, but not drastically; as late as 1887, only 350,000 persons out of a population of four million were qualified to vote, and "signs of fitness and prosperity" were requisites until 1896.

Few things were done hastily in this period of Dutch life. Although the question of school subsidies raised grave problems before the middle of the 19th Century, no solution was found until 1917. Until then the principle of a secular school system was maintained against demands from both Protestants and Catholics for subsidies for their privately maintained schools. The combined pressure from the two groups was too strong to keep down, however, and the eventual compromise granted government subsidies to all schools which met nationally established standards.

Despite the drawn-out school conflict, domestic calm prevailed. In time, hours and working conditions were regulated, the right to strike was accepted and child labor laws were passed. In foreign affairs, the same calm was translated into a determined neutralism. The policy of neutralism was abrogated only once, during the Boer War, when the Dutch openly sympathized with their former countrymen in South Africa against the British. The supreme test came, of course, during World War I. But Holland was able to stay clear.

World War II was different. After five days of brave resistance, the Dutch were overrun. In the wake of the disaster, the "columnization" spirit of *verzuiling* was one of the earliest victims, although it was to return stronger than ever at the war's end. Factionalism disappeared as Catholics, Protestants, Socialists and Communists joined resistance movements. Throughout the nearly five grim years of occupation the Dutch harried the enemy.

The war toll was enormous: 205,000 people died and thousands of homes were destroyed. In their frenetic retreat, the Germans blew up dikes to flood acres of farmland and destroyed what factories they had not already despoiled. The Dutch rose to the new challenge and worked harder than ever to achieve recovery. Before economic stability was fully accomplished, however, Holland had to withstand one more blow—the loss of Indonesia, which in prewar days had contributed as much as 15 per cent of the national income.

SINCE World War I, Indonesian nationalism had been growing. At times it was expressed in Marxist terms, at others in Mohandas Gandhi's passive-resistance principles. During World War II, Queen Wilhelmina had, from her London exile, proposed a postwar conference to discuss bringing the colonies to a commonwealth status "with complete self-reliance and

freedom of conduct" in internal affairs. But by the end of the war, few colonies anywhere were ready to settle for less than full independence. In Indonesia, the years of abuse and exploitation were recalled to help fan the spirit of revolt. After a series of sporadic battles, full-scale fighting between Dutch and Indonesian troops broke out in 1947. The United Nations managed to bring about a cease-fire agreement, but the Dutch broke this in December 1948 with a surprise attack on the Indonesians. World opinion was strongly anti-Dutch, and pressure from the United States and other nations was applied. Finally, as Dutch businessmen saw valuable properties ruined by the Indonesian scorched-earth policy, the government realized that the chances of re-establishing Dutch control were remote. In 1949 the Netherlands recognized the United States of Indonesia as a separate and sovereign nation.

BY Dutch, English and French standards, the Belgians were Johnnies-come-lately in the empire business. And they might not have arrived at all had it not been for the stubbornness of their king, Leopold II, who ruled from 1865 to 1909, and the aggressiveness of an Anglo-American journalist, Henry Morton Stanley. Leopold recognized the potential of the interior of the "dark continent" of Africa at a time when other European powers were so busy bickering with each other they had neither the time nor the inclination to determine the possibilities in the Congo.

How much Leopold could have accomplished without Stanley is questionable. Stanley had returned to Africa after his famous confrontation in 1871 with the lost missionary, Dr. David Livingstone, and had become one of the greatest explorers of the continent. In 1877 he arrived at the mouth of the Congo River on Africa's South Atlantic coast after he himself had been lost to the world for three years on a great journey of discovery into the interior. His report that the Congo ran through most of Central Africa—a fact which suggested that the continent's riches could be carried out by water—so impressed Leopold that he brought Stanley to Brussels.

Leopold acted on his own, not on behalf of Belgium, when he prevailed on several friends to subscribe a million francs to finance studies of trading possibilities and the building of a railroad in the Congo. The project was given an academic veneer with the title Comité d'Études du Haut Congo, but Leopold and his backers had no illusions about studies; they were out for territory. Stanley, leading the committee's expedition, negotiated treaties with native chiefs of the Congo area from Stanley Falls deep in the interior to the Niaru-Kwilu Valley near the Atlantic. Within five years he had accumulated some 900,000 square miles of Africa for Leopold and his associates. The boundaries, according to a joke of the period, were fixed by "explorers' fatigue."

For a while, however, it looked as if no benefits would ever accrue from this vast area. Administration of so much territory was difficult; money to explore, to build a railroad and to pay salaries was not always easy to raise. Time after time, Leopold had to petition the Belgian government for personal loans. Once, in order to assure a favorable response from the parliament, he showed the legislators his will, in which he proposed to bequeath the Congo Free State to Belgium. After 1890, however, the treasure that Leopold had foreseen in Africa began to flow out in the form of rubber and ivory. Maintaining this flow required harsh exploitation of the natives, and Leopold's agents became experts at it. Forced labor and cruel punishment were so widespread that criticism became worldwide.

ALTHOUGH the critics blamed the Belgian king, much of the adverse comment embraced Belgium as well. Sensitive Belgian politicians decided to change world opinion; in 1908 the government took over the Congo.

In reaction to Leopold's regime, the new colonial government undertook reforms on a paternalistic pattern. Education at the lower levels was instituted so that Congolese could handle jobs which required some degree of literacy. But until 1954 no higher education was offered, nor, with a few exceptions, were Congolese allowed to study abroad.

Some Belgians may have deluded themselves into thinking that this policy would keep the Congolese from ever governing themselves. Others may have believed that self-government was a long-term goal anyhow, so it was essential that basic education be universal before the colony went on to higher things. In addition to schools, Belgian policy in the Congo provided for medical services, housing, recreational facilities and churches. These were held out as the rewards for hard work, and whatever one thinks of paternalism, they were in sharp contrast to the floggings which once had been the rewards for lack of toil.

BY the time Belgium's neutrality was violated by Germany in 1914, the Congo was beginning to justify the application of paternalism. Copper, gold and diamonds were being mined, cotton cultivation had been begun and even some cattle ranches had been started. As much as anything else, the wealth of the Congo crowned the steady growth of Belgium itself into an important industrial nation. Internally, the country's development through the 19th Century had in the main paralleled that of the Netherlands. Universal compulsory male suffrage was introduced in 1893, and after 1900 social benefits like workmen's compensation and health insurance were gradually extended to industrial workers.

The modest prosperity which Belgium had acquired was destroyed by the World War I fighting on its soil and by the four years of German occupation. Factories were ruined, 100,000 homes were destroyed, and nearly 50,000 soldiers and civilians were killed. Belgium struggled back to its feet under the inspired leadership of King Albert, but the job was not made easier by reason of the country's possession of the Congo, for its development had languished, and the colony was actually an economic detriment in many of the interwar years. The impact of the Congo on the Belgian economy was felt after World War II, however. Greatly developed during the war, which hardly affected it, the colony was one of the factors which permitted Belgium to recover rapidly. The Congo became an excellent market for Belgian machine goods, and in return Congolese raw materials became the bases for new industries which attracted Belgian investors.

SINCE the Congo had one of the highest standards of living in Africa, Belgians may be pardoned for thinking that their colony was immune to political change. Whatever the reason, the Belgians did not heed the nationalistic rumbling. Their Congo policy had proved workable through two world wars; all the colony seemed to need was more of the same. In 1950 the Belgians instituted a 10-year plan for more roads, railways, airfields, hospitals, homes and schools in the Congo. The key word was gradualism, which amounted to a vague promise that at some unspecified future date there would be a possibility of discussing changes in the Congo's status.

In the Congo, as elsewhere, native leaders appeared who were negative about the vagueness but downright positive about their demands for change. In 1956 Joseph Van Bilsen, a Belgian newspaperman turned political scientist, published an article entitled "A Thirty Year Plan for the Political Emancipation of Belgian Africa." It was the first time a Belgian had proposed a specific timetable.

Despite opposition to the Van Bilsen plan, steps were taken in 1957 and 1958 to prepare the Congolese for self-government. Elections were held in seven of the Congo's biggest cities. These were, in fact, token elections since the offices which the candidates sought were to remain under Belgian control. But in Leopoldville, where the Abako party of Joseph Kasavubu won 62 per cent of the vote on a platform of self-government, the voting was assumed to be the real thing. After the election Kasavubu made a stirring speech. "For a country with 13 million inhabitants, we have 125 university students," he said. "We must wonder why the government has not used all its national and international possibilities after the war for the cultural development of the Congolese." The Belgians were not prepared for such strong words, and after some delay, they gave Kasavubu an "official rebuke" while allowing him to remain in office.

That was the beginning of political consciousness in the Congo, although the Belgians were largely unaware of it. In Brussels, Congolese independence was rarely discussed. At the end of 1958, Patrice Lumumba, who helped form the Mouvement National Congolais, delivered some magic words: "Independence is not a Belgian gift, but a fundamental right of the Congolese." Kasavubu took the same line. A week after Lumumba spoke, rioting broke out in Leopoldville. Congolese independence thenceforth became a major topic of conversation in Brussels. What is more, Van Bilsen's 30-year plan, which once had seemed so short, now seemed incredibly long. To Belgians who had followed the twists and turns of France's relationship with North Africa, the question resolved itself to one thing only: Who wants another Algeria?

IN January 1960, Belgians and Congolese met in Brussels to work out a timetable for independence. The question of years did not even come up; the delegates spoke in terms of months. Lumumba named June 1 as an appropriate date; the Belgian vice premier suggested August 30. As a compromise, June 30 was agreed upon. In the words of Robert Coughlan in his book *Tropical Africa*, "From complacency the Belgian attitude had progressed to misgiving to comprehension to alarm to panic; and the policy that had granted too little too late now gave too much too soon."

One final Belgian attitude has to be recorded as well: relief. Without troublesome colonies to distract them, the Belgians, like the Dutch, could now turn their full attention to European affairs where, in the last analysis, they would find their real future.

A Dutch official (behind desk above), flanked by native notables and a secretary, presides at a trial of two Indonesians about 1870.

The Death Throes of Great Imperial Domains

The thrust of nationalism in Asia and Africa stripped Holland and Belgium of colonial empires which were large and lucrative. In their 350-year rule of the East Indies, the Dutch had carved thriving cities from the jungle and had tapped the islands' vast resources. But they also held tight the levers of government, and their rule, especially in the 19th Century, was often severe. After the dislocations of World War II, the Indonesians, despite Dutch persuasion— and military force—demanded independence. A similar fate overtook the Belgian Congo. The Belgians had turned from exploitation to more enlightened policies, but they still found the Congolese, although tragically unprepared, were aflame with a strong desire to rule themselves.

DUTCH CLUB in Batavia (later renamed Djakarta) serves beer to several Dutch businessmen. The club, called the Sociëteit de Harmonie, was founded in 1805 to provide Dutch specialties for the businessmen and officials so many miles from home.

DUTCH TROOPS ride past weary Indonesians *(left)* during the fighting of 1947. The Dutch claimed their troops were engaged in a "police action," but the U.N. Security Council, believing it a Dutch attempt to hold the colonies, voted for a cease-fire.

DUTCH DEPARTURE is signaled by the removal of a portrait of a former Dutch official *(below)* from the governor-general's palace in Batavia. The palace, with its pillared porch, has become the winter residence of Indonesia's President Sukarno.

THE BELGIAN CONGO, granted independence in 1960, was immediately divided into warring factions

NUCLEAR REACTOR is demonstrated by Monsignor Gillon, rector of the Congo's new Lovanium University. Owned by the university, the reactor was the first to be installed in Africa.

BELGIAN OFFICIALS attend the inauguration *(above)* of Joseph Kasavubu as President of the Republic of the Congo in 1960. The Congo government soon became torn by rivalries.

FRIGHTENED REFUGEES fill the double-decked interior of a U.S. Air Force Globemaster as they are airlifted from the Congo in July 1960 to escape from the rioting Congolese.

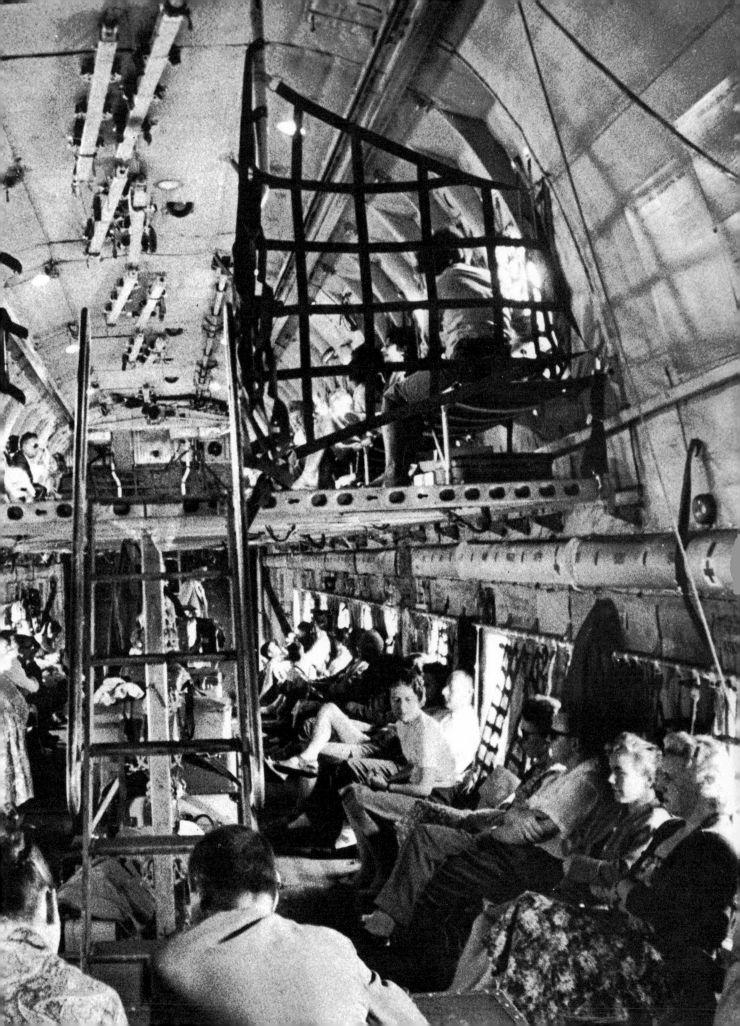

A golden coach carries Holland's Queen Juliana (in window at left) through the packed streets of Amsterdam after her inauguration

in 1948. With her rode Prince Bernhard and their daughters.

4

The Royal Democracies

IT is one of the ironies of current history that at a time of swirling changes, conflicting ideologies, minor wars and the danger of major ones, the institution of the monarchy has gained fresh strength and respect. Not so long ago, as these things are reckoned, royalty was often considered at best an antiquated and useless appendage to modern society, or a danger to democracy that had to be removed. Today kings, queens, princes and princesses are highly regarded as symbols of national unity in their own countries and as good-will ambassadors abroad. Even the charge of anachronism is hardly heard any more.

The change in attitude is due in large part to the growth of parliamentary democracy in the 19th Century and the corresponding decline in royal powers. It also derives from the personalities of most of the monarchs of this century who, free of political responsibility, have accepted the greater responsibility of representing their people in the face of internal division and external danger. Monarchs who neglect the new responsibility are not only out of step with the times, but often off their thrones.

Nowhere in recent years has the role of the modern monarch been dramatized so vividly as in the Low Countries. Queen Wilhelmina of Holland became the symbol and conscience of Dutch resistance while in exile during the painful years of Nazi occupation, and returned after liberation to inspire the early efforts at reconstruction and recovery. Leopold III of Belgium chose to remain on native soil as a prisoner of the Germans where, whatever his motives, he had little influence for either hope or harmony, and found after liberation that his country was so bitterly divided over him that he was forced to abdicate.

TODAY Juliana, the daughter of Wilhelmina, is Queen of the Netherlands and Baudouin, Leopold's son, is King of the Belgians. The difference in their titles derives only from the reluctance of the 19th Century Belgians, remembering their years of outside control, to give Leopold I, their first king, the impression that he held title to the country—or that his successors would. Both are the fifth of their lines to hold their countries' thrones, which in both cases go back only to the first half of the 19th Century—the Netherlands' to its emergence from annexation to France as an independent nation in 1813, and Belgium's to its independence from Holland in 1830.

Each is young; Juliana is in her fifties, Baudouin in his thirties. Each is the nominal head of a state in which policies are determined by politicians whose powers are democratically controlled. Each understands the limits and the potentialities of monarchy in the 20th Century. And after these similarities are noted the differences between the two monarchs, and the two monarchies, are manifest.

The Dutch like Juliana. This is a tribute to her person, not her office, because while the Dutch respected Wilhelmina, they felt little emotional attachment to her until World War II. Juliana maintains the dignity required of her position, but she is also disarmingly informal—and it is just this combination which the Dutch believe is innate in the national character and which they find so comfortable. Juliana does not like to be called "Your Majesty" at unofficial gatherings. People meeting her for the first time are told that she prefers to be called *mevrouw,* the Dutch equivalent of *madame,* but a word which has a comfortable housewifely feeling that the French one lacks. In the country at large she is regularly referred to as Juliana, not as "the queen."

The feeling that Juliana is of them, rather than above them, dates back for the Dutch to the time when she enrolled at the University of Leyden as a regular student. This was a fresh approach for Dutch royalty, and unexpected, since Juliana's education until then had been directed by private tutors at the palace. At Leyden she took courses in Dutch history, international law, religious history and modern Dutch literature. Perhaps more important, she took an active part in extracurricular affairs. She did not commute from the palace, choosing instead to live with several other students.

During her freshman year, she was one of a number of students who anonymously submitted lyrics to be selected by seniors as student song of the year. Her entry won, but it took a letter from the jury to Wilhelmina to convince the queen that favoritism had not been involved. Juliana also wrote and acted in a play based on the Bluebeard story, in which the moral was that modern women are not much different from their grandmothers. In the play Bluebeard was a psychiatrist; Juliana played his wife.

LEYDEN students since her day have regarded Juliana with special affection. When her engagement to Prince Bernhard of Lippe-Biesterfeld was announced in 1936, about 80 Leyden coeds raced around buying flowers and orange decorations, then collected automobiles for a parade to the palace, less than an hour away. Juliana received her unannounced visitors, warmly accepted their offering, introduced

Bernhard to the group and then joined them in singing the Leyden coed song.

Obviously, informality and a friendly disposition alone are not enough to qualify someone as a successful monarch, especially in the face of problems such as those which confronted Holland when Juliana assumed the throne in 1948. Wilhelmina had voluntarily retired as sovereign after 50 years to allow, as she said, younger hands to direct the affairs of the royal family and its relations with the nation. The war had ended, but the monumental job of reconstruction had barely started, the stirrings of Indonesian nationalism had brought a crisis and military action, and the political situation at home had become far from restful as Communists, Socialists, Catholics and Conservatives pushed their separate programs.

WITHOUT the power actually to direct events, Juliana nevertheless has been an important influence on the path which Holland has followed since she became queen. Like her mother she has a deep interest in Dutch affairs and a strong sense of duty. Under the Dutch constitution she is limited to the right to advise, to be heard and to warn. Wilhelmina used these rights wisely and gave Holland what it needed most in time of crisis—a sense of continuity and stability. Juliana does this, too, although it will be some years before her effectiveness can be properly measured against her mother's. It was obvious to Dutchmen during the Indonesian tension, which exacerbated feelings at all levels of the population, that Juliana was reconciled to Indonesian independence. The clues were in the speeches she was called on to make; no cabinet minister, for example, would ask her to make one in favor of a measure she had privately opposed. When she does speak, it is not difficult to detect conviction—or indifference.

Juliana's influence on the sense of national stability and continuity that exists in Holland derives from her ability to emphasize those tendencies that tend to unify the community while ignoring those that push toward disunity.

She herself, in the tradition of the House of Orange-Nassau, is a member of the Nederlandse Hervormde Kerk (Dutch Reformed Church). Since her country's religious division is so strong, no great point is made of this. The Dutch press followed this discreet tradition in 1956 when foreign papers reported that Juliana had taken up—and then rejected—faith healing, and all but ignored the matter.

THE Dutch constitution, which was written when the king's powers exceeded those of the parliament, has had half a dozen formal revisions. These, combined with a vast body of unwritten law, have given the Dutch the kind of democracy most often associated with Britain. One of the constitution's provisions clearly identifies the place of the king (or, as has been the case since 1898, the queen). "The King is inviolable, the Ministers are responsible."

Under such a precise definition of parliamentary democracy, Holland has been able since World War II to change its government—i.e., the composition of the cabinet—nine times without violence or danger to individual freedom. Each government has been a coalition, and until recently each was usually made up of the Catholic party and the Socialist party. In May 1959, however, the Socialists moved into the opposition; whereupon the Catholic party formed a government with the Liberals, a group which opposes too much governmental regulation. But as far as any but the most sensitive or partisan observer can note, matters have proceeded pretty much as they always have. The Catholic party, which started its political life as a conservative group, now has as much of a stake in promoting social legislation as have the Socialists. The Socialists, on the other hand, long ago gave up revolutionary doctrine and are now more interested in appealing to the middle class and to intellectuals. They have succeeded in this to some extent and have even attracted a number of individual Catholics, some of whom hold high party posts.

Minor parties have been a phenomenon in Holland since 1917, when a constitutional election for representatives to the States-General.

Only 14 received enough votes to win at least one seat. The Catholics led with 28, followed by the Socialists with 22. The Communists won four seats, the Political Reformed (a conservative Calvinist party) won three, and the semi-Fascist League of National Rehabilitation and the National Farmer Horticulturist and Middle-Class party were among those which won one seat each. Among the losers were seven Socialist and Labor splinter groups, three Roman Catholic and six Fascist groups as well as candidates who represented such causes as "Justice and Liberty," "National Prosperity" and "Anti-Depression."

Some of the flavor of Dutch political life has gone with the departure of these once strident voices. As all of the Dutch parties today move closer to the main, or middle class, stream of national life, they give the appearance of bland uniformity. What excitement exists in politics is generated by the Anti-Revolutionary party and the Christian Historical Union, once strong forces for Dutch conservatism, but now speaking for a small minority. Staunchly Calvinist, the two parties are a sort of old guard holding hard to principles which most of their countrymen find hopelessly old-fashioned.

EXTREMES of right or left have never had a strong appeal in Holland. After World War I an ill-conceived attempt at a Socialist revolution led to a few riots, but petered out for lack of popular support. Even during the depression, the extremists made no headway. At their strongest, the Communists could not win more than four seats in the States-General. After World War II, because of its members' active resistance record, the Communist party's strength reached a high of 10.6 per cent of the vote and 10 seats. Since then the party has dwindled to almost complete ineffectuality. The Nazi party received 7.9 per cent of the votes cast in 1935; this dropped to 4.2 per cent in 1937 and to 3.7 per cent in 1939. At the desperate points of history, it is clear, most of the Dutch have eschewed the apparently easy

revision instituted universal and compulsory suffrage and also established proportional representation, the system under which political parties are awarded seats in a legislature in proportion to the percentage of votes cast for them in an election. At the depth of the depression, in 1933, when nearly every economic panacea had a political party attached to it, 54 distinct groups entered candidates in the answers in favor of safe, if plodding, progress.

Although over the years Belgian political progress may be considered just as plodding as that of Holland, Belgium's modern history has been marked by more explosive issues, one of which brought into question the throne itself. On July 17, 1951, Baudouin, a few weeks shy of 21, swore "to observe the constitution and the laws of the Belgian people, to maintain their national independence and the integrity of the territory." He had inherited the throne which his father, Leopold III, had abdicated. He had also inherited an accumulation of ill will which, though greatly ameliorated today, can still generate agitated discussion.

AFTER the passage of more than a decade, Baudouin has begun to win some of the kind of admiration the Dutch have for Juliana. The Belgian throne, however, may never come to represent the unifying national force that the Dutch monarchy does. The fault is not Baudouin's, but lies rather in circumstances and the nature of Belgium. "We are a small country," his great-great-grandfather Leopold I once told Prince Metternich of Austria, "but not small in politics."

Baudouin came to the throne after Belgium's politics had kept the country in turmoil for six years. With liberation the Belgians, like all other occupied peoples, took out after those who had collaborated with the Nazis. About 53,000 were found guilty (roughly the same number as in Holland), but the number may not have been as disturbing to many Belgians as the feeling that during the war itself Leopold III had not behaved in the best interests of the nation. Stiff, headstrong and inclined to ignore his ministers' advice, Leopold had never won the affection the Belgians had shown for his father, King Albert, the symbol of Belgian resistance in World War I. When, 18 days after the Nazi invasion of Belgium in 1940, Leopold surrendered his armies and permitted himself to be taken prisoner, he put himself in a controversial position, endangering his chances of ever again exerting leadership over his people.

Leopold took a defeatist "wait and see" stand, and not, as some of his bitterest critics have said, a pro-German one; he truly felt that he could do more within Belgium than in exile. Although German treatment of the Belgians was relatively mild, Leopold's belief not only proved unhappily wrong but appeared to many Belgians to have been willful and evil when his actions were contrasted with those of Wilhelmina. As a prisoner of the Germans, shifted from one place of confinement to another, he was not the symbol of resistance to patriotic Belgians that Wilhelmina was to the Dutch. At the end of the war, he was found near Salzburg, Austria, where the Germans had moved him for safekeeping. Even he himself understood that he could not return to Belgium; his brother, Prince Charles, who had gone into hiding at the suggestion of the resistance in the last months of the war, took over as regent.

IN exile in Switzerland, Leopold continued to nourish his desire to regain his throne. In Belgium he had the support of the Catholics, but the opposition of the anticlerical parties. On March 12, 1950, a plebiscite on the Royal Question—whether or not the king should resume the throne—was held. Leopold won, but the margin was so narrow and such a dramatic reflection of the country's division that he hesitated. Had he persisted it is quite possible that Belgium might have had civil war. Amid riots, and under the prodding of political leaders, Leopold accepted the inevitable, with a slight bit of face saving: he would live in Belgium as king without the minimal constitutional powers of the king; these would be delegated to his son, who would accede to the throne in a year. The country accepted the solution, and on Baudouin's succession a Brussels wit said, "The crisis is dead. Long live the king."

The crisis may have died, but some of the intense feelings it left in its wake are still apparent. Baudouin is more popular than his father was. As a dutiful son he has not, however, rejected his father. At the start of his reign the presence at the palace of Leopold and his wife, Liliane Baels, a commoner whom he married after the death in 1935 of his first wife, Queen Astrid, and later elevated to princess, was resented by anti-Leopold Belgians. Since Baudouin's marriage in 1960 to Doña Fabiola de Mora y Aragón of Spain, however, Leopold has traveled a good deal; he rarely appears at the palace these days. Fabiola's charm has helped Baudouin to relax in public—he was almost pathetically shy and withdrawn when he took the throne—and to gain the affection of Belgians who were against Leopold.

NONE of the three major political parties in Belgium can muster a majority. Except for one four-year period every government since 1919 has been formed by a coalition. The Social Christian party, the name of the Catholic party since World War II, has been the strongest in numbers as well as in representation of all classes of the population. Its greatest bulwark is in Flanders, from which it draws its working-class voters who also belong to the Federation of Christian Trade Unions, the Catholic labor organization. And, not so oddly for Belgium, businessmen and aristocrats also find themselves at home in the Social Christian party.

The Socialist party has long since dropped its militant economic views and recently softened its anticlerical stand. Its members, many of whom are from industrial Wallonia, mostly belong to the non-Catholic trade union, the General Federation of Belgian Labor. The Liberal party, which led the 19th Century fight against state-subsidized Catholic schools, is no longer particularly anticlerical, and in 1961 changed its name to the Party of Liberty and Progress. With 10 to 12 per cent of the vote in each election the Liberals have the strength to form a coalition government with either the Socialists or the Social Christians.

Strangely, with its many diverse interests and associations, Belgium has never encouraged minority parties. Before World War II, the Rexist party, a Fascist group, came into existence. Under clever leadership it exploited discontent among all classes and in 1936 won 21 seats in

the parliament. In 1939 this was reduced to four. Since the war, the strong Socialist party has been a damper on the Communists, who reached a high of 12.5 per cent of the vote in 1946 but subsequently dropped to 1.1 per cent.

Even without the provocation of gadfly minority parties, Belgians can whip up a good political fight on virtually any issue. In 1955, riots and protests by Catholics followed the introduction of a bill sponsored by Socialists and Liberals which called for the construction of new public schools and a reduction of subsidies to parochial schools by 13.5 per cent. The bill was passed, but in 1958 a compromise was reached which gave equal support to both public and parochial schools. Late in 1960 another coalition, between the Social Christians and the Liberals, proposed the Loi Unique, a complicated omnibus bill which would have raised taxes and reduced some social security benefits. A monthlong strike directed by the Socialists failed to prevent passage of the bill but did cause the eventual shelving of some of its provisions, and brought still a third coalition—this time of Social Christians and Socialists.

OTHER matters can also stir up political storms in Belgium. The Flemish movement, for example, started as a literary and cultural revival during the period when Belgium was part of the Kingdom of the Netherlands. Flemish heroes of the past were invoked by young poets and novelists. The Flemish lion from the coat of arms of the counts of Flanders became a symbol to rally around, inspiring a song—entitled "The Lion of Flanders"—and a romantic novel with the same name. The book linked the 14th Century struggle of Flanders against France to the 19th Century fight of the Flemish Belgians against their French-speaking countrymen. The author, with the fortunate name of Hendrik Conscience, may have had some doubts about the effectiveness of his fiction.

He made his position clear in a preface which, with the proper statistical changes, remains as concise a statement of Flemish aims today as it was in 1839: "There are twice as

HONORED EMBLEMS OF TWO PROUD PEOPLES

The rampant lion and strutting cock illustrated here have been for centuries the respective symbols of the two major Belgian groups: the Flemings of the north, and the Walloons of the south. Both symbols have ancient lineages. The lion was taken over by the Flemings from the medieval coat of arms of the counts of Flanders. The cock, first used by the Gauls, has been a symbol of courage in the Low Countries since Caesar's time.

many Flemings as there are Walloons. We pay twice as much in taxes as they do. And they want to make Walloons out of us, to sacrifice us, our old race, our language, our splendid history, and all that we have inherited."

The power of literature was strong. The grievances of the Flemings were investigated by an official commission in 1856 and found to have merit. Its recommendations were adopted by champions of the Flemish cause, but no practical results followed for years. The Liberals, who held power for much of the period, were unsympathetic to Flemish demands. Only when the Catholic party controlled the government—from 1871 to 1879 and from 1884 to 1914—did the preponderantly Catholic Flemings make important progress. In 1890, doctoral theses in Dutch were accepted at the University of Ghent, and before World War I a number of courses were offered in Dutch.

DURING the war, extreme Flemish nationalists, prodded by the German occupation forces, decided they could do better outside the political parties. Many of them—called Activists—became collaborators with the Germans, who rewarded them by making the University of Ghent a Dutch-language institution and by enforcing the language laws which the Flemings had succeeded in having passed but had found largely ignored. Those who supported the Flemish movement but could not work with the Germans were called Passivists.

Following a postwar series of trials of the most flagrant Activists—45 were condemned to death, although the sentences were not carried

out—the Flemish movement picked up steam again. It was directed for the most part by Maximalists, successors to the wartime Passivists, who felt they could accomplish their aims within the accepted political structure. They had the support of King Albert, whose first address to the Belgian parliament after the armistice contained this promise: "In the domain of languages the strictest equality and the most absolute justice will characterize bills which the government will submit."

REFORMS did come between the wars, but neither swiftly enough nor far-reaching enough to satisfy the former Activists. Before World War II, some extremists found a home in Fascist groups, and during the war, with the Nazis. Since then the Walloons' strongest epithet for a Fleming has been "collaborator," but moderates on both sides are not taken in by this—enough Rexists and Nazi collaborators from Wallonia were flushed out to make the charge unfair.

Although the Catholic party has a stronger Flemish character than the Socialist party, both groups make every effort these days to keep a balance. The balancing is comparable, in a way, to the composing of political tickets in New York City, where places must be found for Jews, Negroes, Italians and Irish.

Despite the recent emergence of compromise in political matters, Flemish-Walloon rivalry is still a fact of Belgian life. Compromise will have to become an ingrained national habit before Baudouin may be said to be the ruler of a truly united land.

STEADY-EYED PRINCESS, Wilhelmina appears in a cameo-like photograph taken in 1897, the year before she began her active reign at 18. As queen, she studied statecraft, headed dozens of welfare agencies and invariably visited any stricken area.

Regal Continuity and Persistent Rivalries

The royal families of both Holland and Belgium provide a focus for the patriotism of their peoples. At difficult times in the past, especially during the agonies of World War I in Belgium and World War II in Holland, they rallied the resistance of their countries. Tempering pomp with informality, the present Queen of the Netherlands, Juliana, is highly popular among her subjects, and shy Baudouin, King of the Belgians, is becoming accepted and admired by his volatile people. They remain forces for order and unity in the face of the difficult religious and cultural questions that divide their nations.

AGED QUEEN, Wilhelmina on her 68th birthday arrives *(right)* to witness an elaborate pageant depicting events from her 50-year reign. In the same year, 1948, she abdicated the throne in favor of her daughter, Juliana. Wilhelmina died in 1962.

JOLLY MONARCH, Queen Juliana *(above)* pedals through the Dutch countryside during a tour. The royal limousine had had a flat tire, and she insisted on proceeding by bike. Juliana is the first Dutch ruler to have attended a university publicly.

KING ALBERT I listens as Queen Elisabeth and young Prince Leopold play a violin duet around 1910. Albert led the Belgian fight against Germany in 1914, becoming a hero to his people.

KING LEOPOLD III, who took the throne when King Albert died in 1934, attends a meeting of ex-servicemen in 1939 with his mother and his son Prince Baudouin *(right, in sailor suit).*

ABDICATION is signaled by Leopold *(waving, right)* who bequeathed the throne to Baudouin *(next to him)* in 1951 because of popular bitterness over his 1940 surrender to Germany.

THE BELGIAN ROYAL FAMILY in
*this century has fluctuated erratically
in the affections of its subjects*

KING BAUDOUIN escorts Doña Fabiola de Mora y Aragón
to the festive ball that preceded their marriage in 1960. Fabiola is helping Baudouin to enhance the monarchy's popularity.

CIVIL VIOLENCE erupts in Brussels in 1955 as many thousands of Catholics riot against the Socialist-dominated government's plan to cut state aid to parochial schools. In a five-hour battle, during which the police used fire hoses *(above)*, some 80 people were injured and 1,000 arrested. Recent compromise legislation has reduced controversy over the school problem.

WAVES OF DISORDER *plague Belgium over religious and economic questions*

SIGN-CARRYING STUDENTS stage a sit-down in Brussels *(above)* over the higher taxes and reduced welfare budgets that followed Belgium's loss in 1960 of much of its Congo revenue.

MOUNTED POLICE charge a Brussels crowd also demonstrating against the 1960 tax laws. Riots and strikes erupted in all parts of the country, bringing industry to a virtual standstill.

FLEMISH MARCHERS throw their flags into the air as they protest supposed injustices done them by the Brussels government. Although they have a majority in parliament, the Flemish nurse many grievances against the French-speaking Walloons.

WALLOON EXTREMISTS who want to secede from Belgium and join France hold a rally during the 1962 disturbances at one of the monuments marking the battlefield of Waterloo. The rooster, emblazoned on several flags, is the Walloon symbol.

STREET BATTLE rages in Brussels *(right)* as a phalanx of Walloons tries to destroy a sign carried by parading Flemish. The bitter rivalry between the Walloons and the Flemish has tormented Belgium since the kingdom was founded in 1830.

The center of Rotterdam lies in ruins after the German air bombardment of May 14, 1940. Some 25,000 houses and many historically

important buildings were leveled and 78,000 rendered homeless.

5

Out
of the
Rubble

AT a point in downtown Rotterdam, where the city proper ends and the port begins, stands a grim monument to horror—a statue of a torn, distorted figure, openmouthed in agonized surprise, arms raised in despair and anguish, a jagged hole to mark where the heart has been ripped from the body. The bronze, created by the sculptor Ossip Zadkine, commemorates the destruction of Rotterdam by the Luftwaffe on May 14, 1940. It was a wantonly cruel attack; earlier that day the Dutch had signaled for a truce in which to discuss surrender terms. Four years later the Germans blew up more than a third of the city's docks and destroyed nearly half of the port's machinery and equipment. When Rotterdam was liberated in 1945, some 700 acres had been leveled, 30,000 homes and other buildings had been wiped out and the population had been decimated by death or deportation to Nazi labor camps. Rotterdam's return from the brink of annihilation is one of the most amazing displays of courage, stubbornness and backbreaking work in post-war Europe.

In the course of the war other cities in the Low Countries took severe beatings—Antwerp was battered by V-bombs, Arnhem and Liège were badly damaged by fighting that raged through their streets, and Belgian and Luxembourg cities and towns in the Ardennes area were ruined during the Battle of the Bulge. Their revival has to rank high among the world's postwar achievements. Yet, at a time when the image of the phoenix is often invoked for villages, cities and nations which were brutally used during the war and have since been reborn and rebuilt, the achievement of Rotterdam is all the more remarkable for its application of an ingredient most of the others ignored —imagination. Lewis Mumford, the American architectural and city-planning critic, has found the rebuilding of Rotterdam one of the most exciting efforts of its kind. "Not every [bombed] city rose to the challenge of its destruction as determinedly and as skillfully as Rotterdam," Mumford wrote in his modern classic, *The City in History*. "The main purpose of the city as a meeting place, where a diversity of human functions are brought together, has been admirably carried through. The word 'renewal' is a tame one to describe the resurgence of Rotterdam."

PRAISE of this kind, even from so highly respected an authority as Mumford, is taken in stride by Rotterdammers. By now, they have been made aware that city planners from all over the world have studied their achievement. More to the point, except for a few die-hards who fondly recall old Rotterdam or are offended by a particular piece of sculpture or architecture, the residents enjoy the new city. The concept of enjoyment may be a strange one to American city dwellers; it exists to an extraordinary degree in Rotterdam.

On a recent sunny day—rare enough in Holland to call for some show of high spirits—a Rotterdammer placed a pair of sunglasses on the nose of *Meneer Jacques*, a bronze statue which stands at the corner of the Oude Binnenweg and the Coolsingel, one of the busiest spots in the city. With or without glasses, Meneer Jacques is a source of pleasure; he is the kind of joke Rotterdammers enjoy, a mild one on them. He is the image of the stolid citizen, a man with an air of *eigenwijs* and a touch of *deftig*—a know-it-all who just misses being pompous—and somewhat skeptical about the modern city growing around him. Talk to a Rotterdammer, and invariably he says that Meneer Jacques is a good representation of other Rotterdammers, not himself.

THERE is less skepticism in Rotterdam than Meneer Jacques implies, which may be part of his humor, too. Statues and other art on the streets and in public buildings may mystify, amuse or even offend Rotterdammers, but the art is accepted as part of the new city as if it belonged there and no other place. Naum Gabo's *Construction*, a 40-ton metal abstraction that soars gracefully from the sidewalk in front of a department store designed by Marcel Breuer, may not spell out vitality and dynamic tension to its viewers. Rotterdammers simply call it "the Thing" but, now that it has been defaced by the city's sparrows, feel that it is as much a part of the city as the 100-year-old statue of Gijsbrecht Karel van Hogendorp, a Dutch leader in the post-Napoleonic period, which stands on the steps of the exchange building.

Two wrestling bronze bear cubs in the center of the Lijnbaan, the city's new shopping area, have had their noses shined bright by the approving palms of thousands of children. In the main railroad terminal, a couple frozen in metallic embrace by the Italian sculptor Umberto Mastroianni was called *The Lovers* when the work was originally exhibited by the Rotterdam Art Circle a few years ago. When the city purchased it for the railroad station, the sculpture's name was announced as *Farewell*, a concession to civic sensibility. Nevertheless, as Dolf Welling, a Rotterdam art critic, has said, "public morals would be outraged if such uninhibited farewells actually occurred here."

The Rotterdammer, being above all practical, also enjoys his new city for the benefits he derives from it. And there is palpable evidence that these are far greater than those that were found in the prewar city. The bases for these benefits were devised in secret, worked out in cellars and attics behind blackout curtains while the Nazis still occupied the city. "In those years," a Rotterdam official recalled recently, "we were gradually freed from the memory of what was lost, and it dawned upon us that, even though the tragic destruction of the city's center could hardly be called a blessing in disguise, it nevertheless gave us a rare opportunity to make a fresh start."

That start was made possible by the foresight of the city government which, almost immediately after the Nazi bombing, expropriated the ruins of the bombed buildings and the sites on which they had stood. The city thus became the sole proprietor of 415 acres in the heart of Rotterdam and of 1,552 acres outside the city for future housing and industrial needs. Owners of valuable downtown property did not lose their stake in the future; they were to be compensated on the basis of their property's value as of May 9, 1940, the day before the Nazi invasion, and were given an option to buy new sites at the old price when the city was ready for reconstruction.

ON May 28, 1946, the provisional city council of Rotterdam approved the so-called "Basic Scheme" for the city. Essential to the plan was the banning of industry, except for a few small workshops and service establishments, from the center of town. The number of residences was also reduced to 10,000, a cut of nearly two thirds from the prewar figure. The rest of the new housing was to be built just outside the city. The result is a community with a sense of spaciousness instead of confinement: only 30 per cent of the available space was employed for building; in the old city 55 per cent had been used. Wider roads and public gardens make up the difference. Yet the total available

business space has remained the same, for the planners permitted commercial structures to be built higher than in prewar days. The most striking example of Rotterdam's planning is the Lijnbaan, the shopping area which has not only the bronze bears at play, but live parrots (chained but uncaged on pedestals), flower plots and a variety of outdoor cafés. The entire area is limited to pedestrians only, who thereby find shopping a pleasure. As Mumford wrote, the Lijnbaan is "exemplary in almost every way."

AS important as it was to rebuild the center of the city, that job did not get top priority. Most of Rotterdam's prosperity—and a good deal of the country's, for that matter—has long depended on the port. It was not a difficult decision, then, when the war ended, to start clearing the twisted girders, the sunken ships and the ruined quays and wharves before starting on the city itself. Actual work on the port was under way only five weeks after Rotterdam had been liberated; the plans, like those for the rebuilding of the city proper, had been developed during the occupation.

Within five years the port was fully restored, and during its reconstruction it handled all the traffic that came its way. There was not a great deal of traffic, to be sure, since the rest of Europe was undergoing the same slow rebuilding process. Then, in 1952, the effects of the resurgence of agriculture and industry in the nearby Rhine and Meuse Valleys began to reach Rotterdam in ever-increasing shock waves. That year, more than 40 million tons of goods were carried out of the port by more than 15,000 seagoing ships—figures just short of the prewar highs. By the next year, the old standards had been thrown out.

Today, some 25,000 seagoing vessels and 250,000 barges and other small craft enter and leave the port each year. The more than 90 million tons which pass through Rotterdam annually have propelled the city into first place among European ports, ahead of London, the prewar leader, and represent more than the total annual tonnage of Antwerp, Hamburg and Bremen combined.

Aside from the benefits gained from the general economic explosion in Europe, Rotterdam's present size and anticipated growth are predicated on a single commodity—oil. Europe itself produces very little oil, but needs a great deal of it. As more and more tankers arrived at Rotterdam's docks in the 1950s, changes started to take place along the waterfront. Special petroleum docks were built on the south side of the Meuse, and the land behind them was developed for storage tanks and refineries. Oil now accounts for fully half of Rotterdam's annual tonnage, and the port can handle tankers of 85,000 tons. It will soon be able to handle ships of 100,000 tons.

Oil storage tanks with a capacity of 8.2 million tons have been built, and to speed the fuel on its way pipelines to Germany have begun to supplement barges. More important, perhaps, to the economy of Rotterdam is the incredible growth of refineries and chemical plants. Dow Chemical of the United States, Imperial Chemical Industries of England, Royal Dutch / Shell, Gulf, Esso, Tidewater, Caltex and other new tenants are expected to invest more than one billion dollars in plants and machinery in the Rotterdam area.

LOGICALLY enough, Rotterdammers see the growth of the petrochemical industries in the city as an economic offset to the downswings in port traffic and resultant loss of income which come with the periodic drops in world trade conditions. As a further bulwark against loss of income, plans have been drawn for blast furnaces and steel mills, and for metal industries which will be linked to them. The city is doing all it can to encourage new investment. In 1956, a radar system was installed to lead ships safely from the often fogbound North Sea to the inner docks. In 1957, the city council approved plans for Europoort, an extension of the harbor and its facilities to the Hook of Holland, on the North Sea itself. The Gateway to Europe, as Rotterdam officials have taken to calling Europoort, covers 3,900 acres, of which 2,250 are available for industry.

To provide the skilled labor that will be needed for the newly established industries, the city has organized training schools for adult workers in cooperation with trade unions and employers' organizations. It has also increased the budget for its port training school, where youngsters of 12 and up take four- and six-year courses leading to technical and administrative jobs in the harbor.

It is easy to believe, as most Rotterdammers do, in a promising future. The statuary in the harbor—the broken rows of cranes silhouetted as if created by a single-minded boy with an unlimited supply of Erector sets—rises skyward not in agony, as do the arms of Zadkine's statue, but in triumph.

THE well-being and optimism of Rotterdam are reflected in the rest of Holland; they are new experiences for the Dutch, who savor them all the more for having come so late. The war had devastating effects on Holland. The fighting in the northern provinces lasted a full eight months longer than the struggle in Belgium and in southern Holland. In that last winter of the war, the coldest during the entire occupation, food was so short that thousands died of starvation, and those who survived eked out an existence on a diet of tulip bulbs. Furthermore, the Nazis became increasingly vicious as they fell back in retreat before the Allied forces. Dikes and bridges were blown up, farmlands were flooded, and the last food and pieces of machinery were hauled away. At liberation Holland was reduced to national poverty. Nearly a third of its prewar national wealth had been wiped out.

The recovery of the Netherlands is as impressive as the more publicized "economic miracle" of West Germany. The Dutch accepted wage, price and food controls and a low standard of living so that increases in the national income could be applied to the recovery program. Intelligent application of American Marshall Plan aid—in meeting both immediate needs and long-range expansion—propped the broken economy during the most trying post-war years. And then, ironically, the boom in West Germany had its reaction in Holland—first in the increased shipping to Rotterdam, and then in banking, insurance and overland transportation and eventually in agriculture and industry.

Germany's role in the Dutch economy is accepted with a curious ambivalence in Holland. Adriaan J. Barnouw, a former professor of Dutch Language and Literature at Columbia University, once wrote that Chancellor Otto von Bismarck "used to say that Holland would annex herself to Germany. He was a wiser statesman than Hitler. German music, German science, German poetry were popular in Holland before World War II. Dutch scholars studied at German universities and brought not only German methods of teaching back to their classrooms but the very jargon in which the pundits of Berlin and Heidelberg and Bonn used to expound their learning. . . . Dutch journalists were equally guilty of making a bastard of their mother tongue. . . . Bismarck was right: the Dutch were slowly but surely annexing themselves to Germany. Hitler put a stop to that process."

With memories of the occupation under the vicious Nazi Reichskommissar, Arthur Seyss-Inquart, anti-German feelings after World War II were nowhere stronger than in Holland. Educated people who were completely bilingual refused to speak or read German. News of German wartime atrocities dominated the press. Slowly, as Dutch dependence on German prosperity became apparent, the mood changed. In 1950, Jo Spier, Holland's foremost political cartoonist and a wartime prisoner of the Germans, drew a bitter cartoon

---

EUROPE'S BUSIEST PORTS

The busiest ports in Western Europe are listed below. The figures in the right hand column represent millions of tons transshipped in 1961.

Port	Millions of Tons
Rotterdam	90.1
London	87.8
Antwerp	38.6
Hamburg	29.7
Bremen	14.9
Emden	11.5
Amsterdam	11.2

New York, the world's biggest port, handled 100 million tons of cargo. Rotterdam was second. Close behind were Asian ports like Kobe and Yokohama.

---

commentary on the change. In one panel a German paratrooper descends from the sky, machine gun in hand, while Dutchmen below flee in all directions; in the next panel, the same paratrooper is descending in civilian clothes, briefcase in hand, while the Dutchmen below welcome him with open arms.

The new invasion was not welcomed by all Dutchmen, of course, even by those who felt they had to carry on business with the Germans. Stories of German lack of sensitivity were common in those days. They were generally of the kind told by a factory owner about concluding a sale with a young German who was carried away by his own version of good feeling. "I like doing business in Holland," the visitor remarked. "I enjoyed it here so much during the war."

The anti-German feeling has not entirely disappeared. Volkswagens are by far the most popular automobiles in Holland, but there are still Dutchmen who will not purchase one, or any other German product, and who criticize friends who do. Many Dutchmen boycott coast resorts which cater to German tourists; the result has been that many of these places—the island of Texel and much of Zeeland, for example—have become largely German outposts in the summer. Acting up by German *Halbstarke* —juvenile delinquents, usually on motor bicycles—in Dutch-German border towns does not help matters, either. Dutch outspokenness about the Germans is likely to go on no matter how much business Holland does with its former enemy.

The German occupation was less severe in Belgium than in Holland, but it did intensify anti-German feelings carried over from World War I. Invaded and occupied during that war, Belgium required years to re-establish even the moderate level of prosperity it had enjoyed before 1914. In general, however, anti-German sentiments softened in a glow of prosperity after World War II. The economy was not ruined during the war, and the country received a boost in the immediate postwar years from the sale of Congolese mining products. A currency reform instituted soon after liberation, while painful, slowed down inflation, killed the black market and permitted Belgium to build a gold and dollar reserve, the only country in Europe to do so. Its coal mines, although not the most efficient in the world, were operating, and the coal at least permitted Belgian factories to produce. Luxembourg, with which Belgium had formed an economic union in 1922, had its steel mills rolling at near capacity within months after the Nazis retreated.

FOR years, while most of Europe was wrestling with inflation and shortages, nearly all of the necessities and most of the luxuries were readily available in Belgian stores. American cars, which elsewhere in Europe identified United States government officials, were simply another means of transportation for Belgian businessmen. Prosperity was by no means universal; wages were low and prices high, but because of the free economy Belgian trade unions could, and did, agitate for their share of the country's wealth.

The great disparity between Holland and Belgium threatened to kill negotiations for the proposed Benelux economic union before they were properly under way. Gradually the Dutch closed the gap. In fact, by being forced to build completely modern plants in many industries, the Dutch soon started to produce more efficiently than the prosperous Belgians, who often neglected to improve or replace old and inefficient machinery. In the late 1950s, with Holland making steady progress and Germany and France striding ahead, Belgium went through a recession. Its inefficient coal mines could not compete once those of the German Ruhr regained strength. Labor costs in Belgium,

once among the lowest in Europe, mounted to join the highest. In the Borinage region 57 mines were shut down and 38,000 men laid off. Today, however, Belgian prospects for the future are high, thanks in part to the Common Market, the German boom and the influx of American investments.

Prosperity's effects are visible everywhere in the Low Countries, but perhaps nowhere so dramatically as on the streets and highways. As more and more Dutch and Belgians achieve the great postwar ambition of owning their own cars, traffic problems become increasingly overwhelming. Belgium has 754,000 cars, compared with 110,000 before the war, most of them still German and American makes. Some 605,000 automobiles are now registered in Holland, compared with the 300,000 just before the war and the 29,000 immediately after. Most of the new cars in Holland are small French Citroëns (which the Dutch call the *"eend,"* or ugly duckling), Volkswagens and DAFs, the first Dutch-manufactured cars. Gasoline is expensive, and low fuel consumption and low maintenance costs are greater factors in choice of car than esthetics.

THE large "L" for learner prominently displayed on driving school vehicles is a common sight, and considered fair warning to other drivers, bicyclists and pedestrians. The job of driving instructor in a nation leaping directly from pedal power to the internal combustion engine may be as hazardous as that of coal miner. Highway accidents are on the increase in both countries and the subject of scare headlines in the newspapers, especially on Monday mornings. The Belgians attack the problem directly on the highway itself: they erect a cross draped with black crepe and a sign reading, "For the 15 victims of accidents at the crossing three kilometers from this point," or simply, "Slow down. Twenty-seven people lost their lives last year by going too fast on this curve."

The Dutch have not come to this yet. On the other hand they have a unique traffic hazard against which printed warnings seem useless. An average of 50 cars a year drive into the Amsterdam canals, a problem which is the responsibility of a special branch of the Amsterdam municipal police called the *grachtenvissers* (canal fishermen). Low barriers have been erected at the edges of some canals but they are of no apparent help. The *grachtenvissers* also dispense information on what to do when trapped in a sinking automobile (stay calm, keep car windows closed; when water stops rising in car, open window and swim out).

CANAL survival (automotive division) is not yet a pertinent problem to most Dutchmen. Bicycles have been driven into the canals for years, thus prompting the original creation of the *grachtenvissers*, but special lessons were never considered necessary. Despite the influx of cars, the bicycle is still as ubiquitous as ever. There is roughly one for every 2.6 Dutchmen, the highest number per capita of any country in the world. But the new prosperity has wrought changes in custom and style. Once the sole means of transportation for all but the very rich in Holland, bicycles are now used mainly for short hops—to take a child to kindergarten (by the third grade he will have his own bike), to go to work and school (because automobile parking is a problem and even new buildings provide plenty of bicycle racks), and to walk the dog (a common practice that takes uncommon skill).

The major switch in bicycling is to the motorized version, which the Dutch call a *bromfiets* (buzz bike). Scooters and motorcycles are less common because they are taxed at a higher rate than buzz bikes and are banned from the special bicycle paths in the cities and on the highways. The worst effect of the trend to motors, aside from the noise, is that it has destroyed the dignity which the Dutch, especially elderly women, once brought to bicycle riding. In the past they sat on their bicycle saddles as stiffly and as proudly as if they were in the rear seat of a chauffeur-driven limousine; today they hunch over as if competing in the Tour de France,

the French long-distance bicycling marathon.

The general speed-up in the pace of life has gone hand in hand with the new affluence of the Low Countries. Travel has become popular. Automobile owners start planning for next year's holiday abroad as soon as they are back from this year's. Those without cars sign up for bus or airplane tours, especially to Greece, Spain, Italy and southern France, whose well-publicized sunshine is generally considered the only proper antidote to the Dutch and Belgian climate.

Travel, in turn, has encouraged new appetites; the Dutch, who once considered all foreign cheese inferior to their own Edam and Gouda, are now avid consumers of French Brie and Camembert and Italian Gorgonzola, as well as of other imported delicacies. Refrigerators, television sets and electrical appliances, while far from standard household items in the Low Countries, are advertised with increasing frequency. Dutch and Belgian merchants— and sociologists—believe it is only a matter of time before these move from the luxury to the necessity class.

While some of the established habits of thrift have gone by the board with the coming of the new wealth, the Dutch and the Belgians are not so carried away that they have lost their traditional sense of reality. They are aware that they are no longer able to maintain the posture ascribed to them by the British foreign minister, George Canning, in 1826, when Belgium was part of Holland:

> *In matters of commerce the fault of the Dutch*
> *Is offering too little and asking too much.*

In Europe's 19th Century power struggle, that was the way for a small nation to survive and prosper. In the aftermath of World War II, the Low Countries have learned that survival and prosperity are more likely when the give and take is in better balance. Their commitments to reality, to each other and to the nations with which they are allied economically and politically are not likely to be drowned in a flood of Dutch and Belgian consumer goods.

1951

WRITHING FIGURE with a gaping wound in its torso evokes the horror of the German saturation bombing of Rotterdam. Sculpted by Ossip Zadkine, it is one of the new city's many striking statues.

TIERED BALCONIES decorate a new apartment house *(opposite)* in Rotterdam. The balconies have railings in front, but sides of frosted glass. Rotterdam has built more than 55,000 apartments since 1945.

Frightful Destruction and Creative Rebuilding

Rotterdam has been a spectacular leader in the reconstruction and recovery of the Low Countries since World War II, a symbol of the economic growth of the entire area. Virtually the entire center of the city was leveled by German bombers in 1940, and four years later the German armies, facing defeat, wrecked Rotterdam's port. But with courage and intelligence the people have rebuilt their city. Today it is a model of urban planning to the entire world.

*ROTTERDAM HARBOR surges
with activity as the principal port
of booming Western Europe*

STUBBY TUGBOAT named the *Inga Heine (above)* bustles through the waters of Rotterdam harbor. The port has 180 tugs busy jockeying its yearly traffic of some 25,000 seagoing ships.

FLOATING CRANES transfer a ship's cargo into a lighter *(far right)* for shipment to shore. In the distance is an observation tower which overlooks recently built port installations.

VARIED CARGOES, red oil drums in a barge and Mercedes-Benz automobiles on railway cars, await shipment at Rotterdam. Rotterdam handles some 200,000 inland craft each year.

MASSIVE LEGS support heavy-duty cranes *(below)* on a Rotterdam dock. The port has 25,000 yards of dockside for sea-going vessels and will soon accommodate 100,000-ton tankers.

*PROSPERITY is
reflected in the growing
cities and the peoples'
increased leisure*

FLOWERY PROMENADE in rebuilt Rotterdam *(opposite)* combines the virtues of a shopping center and a park, making the center of the city inviting rather than repellent.

WINDOW DISPLAY of shoes attracts a child *(right)* out for a Sunday stroll in Esch-sur-Alzette, Luxembourg. Luxembourg, its industry booming, has almost no unemployment.

LEAFY PARK in Tournai, Belgium *(below)*, provides an ample play area for children. Tournai was badly damaged in World War II, but is once more a prosperous manufacturing center.

A visitor to the Hospital of Saint John in Bruges studies the Shrine of Saint Ursula, a magnificent reliquary decorated with jewel-lik

...aintings of Ursula's life by the 15th Century master Hans Memling.

6

Masterpieces for a Small Audience

THE dictators of literary fashions have rarely devoted much attention to writers in the Low Countries. With few exceptions—Maurice Maeterlinck, who won the Nobel Prize in 1911; Georges Simenon, the prolific author of psychological thrillers; and Anne Frank, whose wartime diary has become internationally famous—Belgian and Dutch writers are little known beyond their borders. Most people are surprised to learn that Maeterlinck and Simenon are Belgians. A good deal of the ignorance can be attributed to the problem of language. Low Countries writers who use French are considered to be Frenchmen, which is understandable, since many of them achieved their success in Paris. Those who write in Dutch are rarely translated. Further, Belgian writers are almost without honor in their own country. Belgians did not recognize Simenon as one of their own until he was acclaimed abroad.

Despite the obstacles, literature in the Low Countries has had a lively past and is enjoying an exciting present. There have been enough talented writers in the Low Countries to support the contention of Adriaan van der Veen, a young Dutch critic, that "a large audience is not a necessary condition for creating a masterpiece." As early as the Middle Ages, when Latin was the language of scholars, Low Countries writers were trying to reach their audience, however small, in the language of the people. Dutch literature started to develop in the Southern Netherlands (today's Flemish area of Belgium) and gradually moved north. In the course of this movement, two distinct elements started to become evident—buoyant, lyrical poetry and prose which explored deep human emotions, and biting social criticism which often invoked humor to make its point. Both elements remain clearly distinguishable in the literature of modern Belgium and Holland.

IN the critical tradition, Dutch and Belgian writers have rarely been content simply to reflect the society in which they lived, as some of the better-known Low Countries painters have done, but have used their art to criticize, to protest, to caricature and, most of all, to suggest that society and its institutions can be altered. One of the earliest Dutch stories, *Van den Vos Reynaerde (Reynard the Fox)*, puts an outcast from society in the role of protagonist and hero.

The Reynard stories go back to the 10th Century, when they probably were compiled by monks. By the time they were committed to Dutch by a 13th Century Flemish poet known as Willem, the heroes and villains had French and Dutch names, reflecting the Low Countries language split. Reynaert the fox, Isengrim the wolf, Grimbert the badger, Bruin the bear are Dutch; Noble the lion, Beline the ram and Chanticleer the rooster are French. Originally told in rhyme, the stories had great appeal for the masses. They parodied chivalry and feudal institutions and satirized the rich, the courts and the clergy. Reynard, the sly little fox who always outwitted the powerful wolf, bear and lion, found strength in his physical weakness.

He used the contempt the others had for him to trap them again and again. Like the heroes of much of modern fiction, Reynard was an outlaw, an outsider, and the comedy of his story was thus invested with tragedy.

The Dutch version became the model for all later recountings of the story. It soon went through many more translations—Low German, High German, Danish, Swedish, Icelandic, English and Latin.

WHILE Reynard was undergoing multiple language changes, Dutch writers were attracting wide audiences with mystical prose and poetry. Jan van Ruusbroec, the best of the Dutch prose writers of the Middle Ages, chose a religious life when he was 15. His writings, which were translated into Latin, High German and the dialects of Gelderland, Cologne and the upper Rhine, probed the roles of God and man with intense feeling. The influence of Ruusbroec and Hadewijch, an aristocratic lady who expressed her religious feelings in visionary prose and lyrical poetry, pervaded the Low Countries in their own lifetimes.

Another major triumph of Low Countries literature is the 15th Century morality play *Elckerlyc*, known in English as *Everyman* and in German as *Jedermann*. The plot itself was centuries old before an anonymous author from the Southern Netherlands put it into play form. *Elckerlyc* won immediate popularity after its first showing at a *Landjuweel* in Antwerp, one of many annual competitions for playwrights. Landjuweelen were sponsored by local Chambers of Rhetoric, whose members organized performances in the provinces of Flanders, Brabant, Holland and Zeeland. Each year, the chamber of the host town established a theme for the contests: "What is man's chief artistic inspiration?" for example, or "What is, in dying, man's greatest consolation?" Playwrights maintained the writers' prerogative to denounce society's ills and frequently took the occasion to criticize secular power by depicting popular grievances. Often, church fathers were alarmed at what they considered examples of heresy. But for the most part, the Landju-weel plays made obvious moral points which had complete church approval.

Of the thousands of plays that must have been written in the Low Countries, *Elckerlyc* is today the best known. The search of Everyman for a companion to accompany him to God's judgment seat, where he has been fetched by Death, would have been difficult for medieval audiences to misinterpret, since its criticism of man's behavior on earth was decidedly explicit. Fellowship assures Everyman that he will go with him "were it to hell," but draws back when he finds he cannot return from this trip. Property rejects Everyman's request with the question, "Did you think I would follow you beyond the world?"

Rejection follows rejection; even Good Works is too weak to make the trip. At last Contrition takes Everyman to Confession, who purges him. As a result Good Works regains his strength, provides Everyman with the robe of Remorse and bids Wisdom, Strength, Beauty and the Five Senses to stay by his side. They accompany Everyman to the edge of the grave, leaving him only at the last moment. The happy ending is announced by Contrition:

> *The heaven is open wide*
> *Where Everyman shall now abide.*

Aside from Reynard and Everyman, and despite the growth of printing, little of international importance in the Low Countries was produced in the language of the people during the 15th and 16th Centuries. Scholars abounded, but they wrote in Latin. During this period, however, Low Countries singers and composers created the Netherlands School of Music, whose polyphonic style dominated Europe.

A return to the language of the people came when the northern provinces won their independence from Spain. In the golden age, metaphysical poets like Pieter Cornelisz Hooft and Constantijn Huygens wrote of love in rhythmic verse. Joost van den Vondel, whom the Dutch consider their Racine, composed poems and plays in classical style but was never as popular as his contemporary, Jacob Cats, who wrote poetic homilies about everyday life. In Amsterdam, where the burgomasters gave support to the theater, playwrights flourished. Traveling troupes played throughout the area. Gerbrand Bredero, a talented playwright and poet who wrote with an earthiness which makes his work easily enjoyable today, once said that he had been "guided by the painter's maxim that the best artists are those who come nearest to life."

WHETHER or not they came near to life, no Dutch or Belgian writers of distinction appeared from the golden age until the 19th Century. In Belgium, the literary revival started with independence from Holland and the beginnings of the Flemish movement. Jan Frans Willems, a poet often called the father of the movement, generated interest in Flemish folk songs and in the creation of Flemish literature. Guido Gezelle evoked the medieval writers of Flanders in a mystical poetry which inspired a new generation of Flemish lyricists and is still widely read. Oddly enough, the best-known work of the period, *The Legend of Ulenspiegel*, although Flemish in subject matter, was written in French. The story, with overtones of *Reynard the Fox*, was about the rogue and scoundrel as folk hero. Ulenspiegel, as depicted by his creator, Charles de Coster, roams the countryside with his companion, Lamme Goedzak, outwitting the 17th Century Spanish overlords.

By the start of the 20th Century a few Dutch and Belgian writers had made a reputation outside the Low Countries. Maurice Maeterlinck started his career as a poet, turned to the theater (where he is best known for *The Blue Bird* and *Pelléas and Mélisande*), wrote essays and was awarded the Nobel Prize for Literature, the only Low Countries author to win that honor. Emile Verhaeren's poems glorified his native Flanders in universal terms and found a wide audience. (Like De Coster, both Maeterlinck and Verhaeren, though Flemish, wrote in French.) In the Netherlands, Edward Douwes Dekker won literary and political fame with *Max Havelaar*, his criticism of Dutch colonial policy. The late 19th and early 20th Century also produced the Dutch writer Louis Couperus, whose abilities were so varied and great that the Dutch call him their Proust, their Galsworthy or their E. M. Forster. Couperus probed the psychological impact of colonialism on Dutch life and wrote brilliantly of the decadence of upper-class life in The Hague.

The immediate prewar predecessors of today's Dutch and Flemish writers, and still a major influence on them, were connected with a publication called *Forum*, which jabbed incisively at complacency and parochialism. Its editors, Menno ter Braak and Charles Edgar du Perron, brilliant literary and social critics, died during the first days of the German occupation of Holland. Ter Braak committed suicide because he could not stand the prospect of living under the Nazis, and Du Perron succumbed to a heart attack. Simon Vestdijk, one of *Forum's* most prolific writers, is a link between the prewar and postwar generations. He is called "the magician" because he writes so well on so many subjects, from the history of religion to modern life. Hendrik Marsman, a *Forum* poet who also died in 1940—on a ship torpedoed by the Germans off Bordeaux—is probably read more by young Dutchmen and Flemish Belgians today than when he was alive. Others of his generation who are still popular are mystical poets like A. Roland Holst and Martinus Nijhoff. Jan-Albert Goris, a Belgian who writes in Dutch under the pen name of Marnix Gijsen, lives in the United States but has a large following in Belgium and Holland for his poems and novels.

LIKE their contemporaries in other countries—England's "angry young men" and America's "beats"—the postwar Dutch and Belgian writers show great sympathy for the outsiders in their society, just as the authors of *Reynard the Fox* did centuries earlier. They see no merit in the bourgeois values of their elders and mock them with grim realism and biting humor. More than anything else, the humor, a modern revival of the Flemish exuberance

found in *Reynard the Fox* and the 16th and 17th Century paintings of Bruegel, Hals and Steen, is a distinctive characteristic of much of modern Low Countries writing.

The literary ambition of Louis Paul Boon, a Belgian who writes in Dutch, and one of the most important of the Low Countries postwar writers, is "to kick a conscience into man." Boon can tell his readers that his work is "a black snowball that grows ever bigger and more sombre and will topple into the ravine ahead of a disintegrating society," and it often seems to be just that. But Boon also makes his point by invoking the tales of Reynard or by making a hero out of a legendary 18th Century Flemish bandit who indulges in practical jokes as he battles authority. The humor often strengthens the pessimism with which the young writers in the Low Countries view the current scene. Boon's bandit, who formed his gang for the idealistic purpose of fighting oppression, is eventually defeated. His own followers succumb to the follies and avarice of society and quarrel among themselves.

AMONG the most popular and the most pessimistic of the Low Countries writers is Willem Frederik Hermans, who teaches physical geography at the University of Groningen. In an early Hermans novel, *I Am Always Right*, the hero is a Dutch soldier who returns embittered to Holland after fighting with the Dutch army in its futile attempt to suppress the Indonesians after the war. Holland, he finds, is conducive to claustrophobia, and its people are condemned to pettiness to maintain an order which is not worth saving. Hermans' *The Dark Room of Damocles* takes place during the occupation; in it, fidelity and heroics are scorned, evil and injustice triumph; there is no hope, only despair. The resistance man who is the book's protagonist is worse off after liberation than he was during the occupation.

The popularity of writers like Hermans, especially among the young, indicates a sharp—and to many older people disturbing—change in the Dutch attitude toward the occupation experience. In 1947, Anne Frank's diary was discovered and published in Holland as *Het Achterhuis (The Attic)*. Its moving account of the life of a Jewish family hiding in a garret in Amsterdam to avoid capture by the Nazis was an immediate success in Holland. The sensitivity and restrained emotions of the young author —who patently did not intend her diary to be published—made it by far the best of the deluge of postwar books on the occupation. Most were poorly written personal accounts or potboiler novels. They were, however, reminders of the suffering and heroism which took place, of the hopes that had sustained much of the nation.

THE disillusion that followed for some of the older writers was accompanied by the coming of age of the younger ones, who had missed the war experience and did not have any illusions to begin with. All they could see was a small country with too many people, whose numbers and values were becoming more and more stifling to the spirit. What they felt was not entirely new to Dutch writers; Arthur van Schendel, one of the finest prewar writers, had said, "Life is suffocating here."

The works of young Low Countries writers are rarely transformed into feature films, as are those of their English counterparts. Dutch and Belgian film makers have, however, created a number of first-rate documentaries. These shorter works have many advantages over feature films for Dutch and Belgian producers. Their reduced length, the absence of large staffs and the lack of paid actors and actresses make them economically feasible. In addition, they are more readily acceptable abroad because most of them can be turned out with commentaries in any language desired, thus dispensing with annoying subtitles. Dutch and Belgian documentary producers have won prizes at most of the major film festivals in Europe quite out of proportion to their limited output.

The first of the Low Countries film men to be recognized abroad was Joris Ivens. His *Zuiderzee* and *Regen (Rain),* which he produced at home, demonstrated fine talents, as

THREE WIDELY INFLUENTIAL THINKERS

Among the many great scholars and thinkers that have been produced in the Low Countries, three stand out for the power of their works and their long-lasting influence.

THOMAS A KEMPIS

Thomas à Kempis' *The Imitation of Christ* is the Christian world's most-read piece of devotional literature aside from the Bible. Thomas à Kempis was a 15th Century monk who spent most of his 91 years in a monastery in Zwolle, Holland. *The Imitation of Christ* is a plea for humility and the renunciation of all worldly vanities.

DESIDERIUS ERASMUS

Erasmus was born in Rotterdam (or possibly Gouda) about the year 1466. Before his death in 1536 he had become probably the most influential and admired writer and scholar of his time. He was first of all a humanist, a leader in the small band of men who, throughout Europe, sponsored the revival of learning which characterized the Renaissance. One of Erasmus' major works is his translation of the New Testament. This task grew out of his conviction that true Christianity was hidden by a thick overlay of dogma and should be purified by a return to the Bible. His 3,000 or more letters give a matchless picture of his mind and his times. Most remarkable of all, for his time, was Erasmus' faith in reason, which is clearly shown in his famous satirical masterpiece *The Praise of Folly*.

BENEDICTUS DE SPINOZA

The philosopher Spinoza was born in Amsterdam in 1632 into a family of Jews that had fled the religious persecution in their native Portugal. As a young man, Spinoza had to earn a living by grinding optical lenses (glass dust in his lungs killed him at 45), but he still managed to formulate, most notably in his *Ethics,* one of the most complete metaphysical systems ever conceived. His system is complex, but at its base lies the simple proposition that God exists only in His creations —that all Nature *is* God—and that man's highest good is to seek knowledge of this Nature. Knowledge, in effect, replaces faith. Such rationalist ideas naturally struck Spinoza's contemporaries as heretical, but despite the *Ethics'* severe method (it reads much like a geometry textbook) his love for the God that he conceived in every created thing plainly shines through.

have some of the films he has made abroad. John Ferno took his apprenticeship with Ivens and has by now surpassed him. His *Isle of Faith* is a moving account of the ordeal of Walcheren after the Allies bombed its dikes.

In the same tradition, and with the same respect for simple Dutch people and ways, Herman van der Horst has filmed whalers and herring fishermen at work. Bert Haanstra is more the poet than the reporter; his best-known film is *Mirror of Holland*, which shows the country as it is reflected in its canals. Paul Haesart and Henri Storck, whose *Rubens* is considered one of the finest camera studies ever made of a painter's work, and Étienne Périer, whose *Bernard Buffet* was well received, are the best known of the tiny group of film makers who have remained in Belgium.

Unlike the modern writers, the Low Countries film makers have not used their medium for social criticism. The Holland and Belgium they depict is made up of landscapes, city streets, people at work, at play and in times of crisis—scenes that have fascinated Dutch and Belgian painters for centuries. In order to keep working, many of the film men have had to make movies abroad. In these, their technical skills are always evident, but when they shoot on home soil or water, extra elements—of love, sympathy, understanding—are invariably added. The results are not only fine films, but in their own way and for their own time a representation of the Holland and Belgium that was familiar to the great painters of the past and is, perhaps, the Holland and Belgium that the angry young writers would like to find.

THE return of Dutch and Belgian film makers to the faces and places that inspired painters during the golden ages of Flemish and Dutch art is not very different from the invocation of the tradition of *Reynard the Fox* by Low Countries writers. A continuity, however tenuous, is apparent. But, oddly enough, modern Dutch and Belgian painters appear to have broken, momentarily at least, the ties with their great predecessors.

After the incredible outburst of creativity in the 16th and 17th Centuries, music and painting in Holland and Belgium went into decline. Art revived near the end of the 19th Century with Van Gogh and a group of painters called The School of The Hague, who consciously returned to Rembrandt and his contemporaries for inspiration. Music returned as a performing art at about the same time.

Amsterdam's Concertgebouw orchestra became world-famous. Its technique remains highly praised. But with the exception of a few artists like César Franck and Willem Pijper, Low Countries composers do not receive a wide hearing. The painters had a different problem. Except for students of art history or inveterate museumgoers, few people recognize members of The Hague School, whereas most beginners in art-appreciation classes can identify a Van Gogh. And he is better known for his sun-sprayed paintings of southern France than for the dark, moody Dutch peasants of Brabant he first painted.

VAN GOGH may represent the initial break with the past which persists today in Dutch and Belgian art. Although several painters in the early 20th Century—notably George Hendrik Breitner—found inspiration in the canals, streets and buildings of Amsterdam, those who followed won acclaim with art that is less easy to classify. James Ensor's imaginative, surrealist works caused one critic to say, "There *is* a Flemish color, a Flemish palette, there is a Flemish vision of the universe." But Piet Mondriaan, who founded the movement called *De Stijl* (The Style) and who may have gone as far as it is possible to go in abstract painting, would not evoke that kind of reaction. The only thing the two artists have in common, aside from their Low Countries origin, is their seeming distance from Dutch and Belgian artists of the past.

Since the end of the war, painters in Belgium and Holland have experimented as freely as their contemporaries in the United States, England and France, and it is still too early to make any judgments on the new work. Yet an argument can be made that the very experimentation, the search for new means of expression with brush and color, may be closer to the tradition of Bosch, Bruegel and Rembrandt than an imitative portrait or landscape is. If this is so, then Van Gogh, Ensor and Mondriaan have not repudiated their heritage at all, but have maintained it.

In a characteristic painting, Pieter Bruegel places Joseph and Mary (seated on a donkey, foreground) in a busy Flemish village.

Towering Mastery of Brush, Palette and Pigment

The glories of Dutch and Flemish painting of the 15th through 17th Centuries are rivaled only by Italian art of the Renaissance. Flowering first in the great altarpieces and portraits of the Van Eycks and their followers, it bloomed in the fantastic visions of Bosch and the village scenes of the elder Bruegel. Then, in the 17th Century, thousands of fine canvases were produced by such artists as Rubens, Van Dyck, Hals, Vermeer, Van Ruisdael, Hobbema and, of course, the supreme Rembrandt. Landscapes, portraits, religious scenes, homely interiors—all flowed from what may have been the largest group of masters ever to be at work at one time. More recently, this creative drive was reawakened in the work of men like Van Gogh and Ensor.

PRECISION of brushwork marks a detailed double portrait *(opposite)* by Jan van Eyck, an early Flemish painter. Executed in 1434, the work is thought to commemorate the wedding of an Italian merchant, Giovanni Arnolfini.

LIGHT bathes a richly robed young lady admiring her pearls *(above)* in a serene portrait by Jan Vermeer, a superb Dutch artist of the 17th Century.

GAIETY radiates from a ruddy fisherboy *(left)* painted by Frans Hals about 1635. Hals loved to catch with bold strokes the faces of working people.

HIERONYMUS BOSCH, best known for his hellish landscapes crowded with monsters, evokes a deep humanity
in a picture *(above)* of Christ being crowned with thorns.

PETER PAUL RUBENS shows his love of bright colors and
his ability to give his forms enormous energy in the dramatic *Last Supper (right)* which he painted around 1620.

BRILLIANT LIGHT floods the robes and the aged face of the Prophet Jeremiah as he laments the destruction of Jerusalem. Rembrandt's portraits seem to probe to the depths of the soul.

DEEP SHADOWS surround the Virgin and Child and the shepherds who pay homage to the newborn Christ *(left)*. The artist's dramatic use of light increases the scene's mystery and wonder.

TORMENTED DUTCHMAN, Vincent van Gogh (1853-1890) is thought one of the greatest of modern artists for such vivid and swirling canvases as *Cypresses (opposite)*, painted in 1889.

HAUNTED BELGIAN, James Ensor (1860-1949) filled etchings like *Death Pursuing the People* (owned by New York's Museum of Modern Art) with nightmare visions of demons and slaughter.

7

Water, Water, Everywhere

A DUTCHMAN recently compressed the national goal of Holland into one sentence: "It is to possess land where water wants to be." This is an oversimplification, of course, yet it carries an essential truth. The Dutch have reshaped their natural boundaries in ways that no other nation has ever attempted. They have been doing it since their own prehistory, and they now project it half a century and more into the future, knowing that even beyond that they will still be at it.

Aside from the sheer physical statistics involved—the creation of 550,000 acres of land in the former Zuiderzee, for example—the long

contest with the sea has made permanent marks on the Dutch way of life. It has brought drastic social changes; it has made farmers out of fishermen, industrial workers out of farmers; it has caused the movement of people from ancient, settled communities to slick, modern, thoroughly planned cities. And it has had a profound effect on the Dutch national character. A good deal of the courage, the tidiness, the humor, the smugness and the conservativeness often associated with Dutchmen derive from Holland's unique adventure with nature.

If geography could not be altered by men, the Netherlands as we know it today would not exist. Two fifths of the country—containing more than half its people, and the cities of Amsterdam, Rotterdam and The Hague—would be under water if it were not for the intricate network of dikes, dams, sluices and pumps created and maintained by the Dutch. All Dutchmen are aware of this, although by now they tend to take it for granted, except when reminded by a tragedy of the proportions of the 1953 flood in southwestern Holland which killed 1,800 people and destroyed or damaged nearly 50,000 homes. The job of reclaiming land from the water and keeping water away from the land is carried out by experts who rarely use emotional phrases to discuss their activities. Thus, one of man's most dramatic achievements often goes unnoticed at home.

FOREIGNERS, however, never fail to be impressed, and frequently take to superlatives to record their reactions. The widely traveled British novelist Hammond Innes, for instance, calls the enclosing dam which transformed the salt-water Zuiderzee into the fresh-water IJsselmeer "the biggest single project achieved by man since the building of the Great Wall of China." Napoleon, when confronted with the sight of 860 windmills turning to keep an area dry, simply said, "Without equal."

The Dutch struggle with the sea was already well under way when Pliny, the Roman historian, described it in 50 A.D. "In the north," he wrote, "we have now seen the tribes of the Chauks [Frisians]. . . . In their region the ocean pours out over a vast stretch of land, at two intervals by day and by night, in a tidal wave so enormous that this eternal struggle in the course of nature makes one doubt whether the soil belongs to the land or to the sea. A miserable people lives there on high hills or on elevations, which they throw up with their own hands to a height which they know from experience to be that of the highest tide, and on these spots they have built their huts. They are like seafarers when the water covers the surrounding land, like shipwrecked people when the waves have retreated."

The elevations, or *terpen,* were the first response of the Dutch to their environment, and they built more than 1,000 of them, some of them 30 feet high and 40 acres in area. None of the ancient *terpen* exists in its original form, but modern Dutch farmers are still grateful to their ancestors because the mounds were built of waste matter like manure, ashes and rotting timber which has made for very fertile land.

In time, the early inhabitants of the Low Countries also devised a method to keep back the sea: the dike. The first dikes may have been clay walls tamped down by human feet and animal hoofs. Whatever they were made of, they were not very effective. They were built for average high tides and so were useless in storms, and they eroded quickly on the side facing the sea. Over the years some of the faults were corrected and new construction materials were found—mud, seaweed and reeds formed a popular combination. Soon the builders went beyond purely defensive measures. They learned to control the flow of water by the proper placement of dams. And they found that by surrounding parcels of land with dikes and installing a system of sluices to permit the discharge of excess water, they could gain arable territory. Between the Eighth and 13th Centuries a 12- to 30-mile-wide strip of land on Belgium's North Sea coast was thus transformed from salty swamp into fine farmland, today among the best in the country. With no remaining swampland, Belgium ceased its reclamation efforts. But from the Eighth Century on, new dikes were erected at a rapid rate all over Holland.

FRIESLAND was completely diked in by the year 1000, although it may be a commentary on the confidence the Frisians had in their handiwork that churches and monasteries were invariably built on *terpen* through the 13th Century. By then the fame of the dikes of the Low Countries had become international; in Italy the poet Dante could mention them casually in his epic *Divine Comedy* in the assurance that the reference would be readily understood:

Just as the men of Flanders anxiously
Twixt Bruges and Wissant build their bulwarks
wide
Fearing the thrust and onset of the sea.

Despite dikes, dams, sluices and windmills—introduced in the late 13th Century to power water pumps—"the thrust and onset of the sea" has remained a constant threat. Until the start of World War II, in fact, Holland's profit and loss statement on its dealings with the sea was still being written in red ink. Between the year 1200 and the late 1930s the sea, by chewing away at the shoreline, increasing the size of the Zuiderzee and creating the Waddenzee to the north of it, had destroyed about 1.4 million acres of land. In the same period the Dutch, by diking their shores and rivers and pumping lakes dry, had reclaimed a little less than 1.3 million acres. Not until the enclosing dam was thrown across the entrance to the Zuiderzee in 1932 could Holland take its first giant steps toward getting ahead of the sea. The Wieringermeer polder of 49,000 acres was drained in 1930, and it was completely colonized and cultivated in 1941. (A polder, so called after the Frisian word *pol*, or protrusion, is a piece of usable and habitable land created by diking and then draining a water-covered area.) The Northeast polder of 119,000 acres was drained in 1942, and recently reached its full housing and population level. When the last of the five polders in the IJsselmeer is completed in 1978, the Dutch will show a net profit of some 450,000 acres since the start of the 13th Century.

This does not seem a great deal for nearly 800 years of work—except when the alternatives are understood. The Dutch, having been exposed to the alternatives—scores of disastrous floods have been recorded since the one which killed 50,000 people in Friesland on December 14, 1287—can make no choice except to hold back the sea. About 1570, what had been for the most part a haphazard approach to that problem became articulated as a planned response to a national need. Andries Vierlingh, one of the greatest of the Dutch dike masters

(officials in charge of the upkeep and repair of dikes), wrote in a classic work entitled *Tract on Diking* that "the foe outside must be withstood with our common resources and our common might, for if you yield only slightly the sea will take all."

Vierlingh was an angry man who not only understood the national problem but had little patience with those who did not or who would not work to solve it. Having himself worked on the dikes he had scorn for officials without practical experience. Dike masters, he wrote, "must be men used to hard work from childhood, men who have greased leather boots on their legs and who are able to withstand a rough climate. Because in time of storms, rain, wind, hail and snow they must be able to persevere." His cure for officials who knew as much about dikes "as a sow about eating with a spoon" was to outfit them with boots "right up to their groins" and have them spend a day in the mud of the tidal flats.

VIERLINGH was the pioneer of defensive measures against the water; Jan Adriaanszoon, who was born in 1575, four years before Vierlingh died, put the Dutch on the offensive. He perfected the methods for draining large lakes in order to create polders of a size to support entire communities. Among other rewards he received during his lifetime was the nickname Leeghwater, meaning "empty of water," and he liked the name so much that he officially adopted it. Leeghwater wrote the *Haerlemmer-Meer-Boek* in which he advocated the draining of the Haarlemmermeer, the country's largest *meer*, or lake, by means of dikes and 160 windmills. His idea caught the public imagination—the book went through 17 printings—as did one of the key sentences in the book: "The draining of lakes is one of the most necessary, most profitable and most holy works in Holland." Although Leeghwater had already shown the way by draining a smaller *meer* called De Beemster in 1612, Dutch officials were not ready for anything as ambitious as the deep Haarlemmermeer. By the time it was drained more than two centuries later, in 1852, steam power instead of windmill power was being used for the polder pumps, which certainly made the job easier. Modern hydraulic engineers believe, however, that Leeghwater's plan would have worked. In tribute to his foresight, one of the three pumping stations which keep the Haarlemmermeer territory dry has been named for him.

LEEGHWATER'S major contribution to the Dutch water-control arsenal was his artful use of the windmill. For his Beemster project he used 40 of them. Until his time single mills had been used to remove water from swamps or tiny polders. The turning sails operated scoops which lifted water a maximum of five feet in most cases; in the 17th Century, a worm or screw pump was developed which permitted water to be raised 16 feet.

However high the water was lifted, it was deposited into drainage ditches called *boezem,* where it could be either stored for use during a dry spell or permitted to run into a river or the sea, a practice still followed today. Leeghwater arranged his mills and ditches at increasingly higher levels and so was able to raise water from fairly deep lakes. His success prompted a number of businessmen to undertake similar projects—the possibilities of profits in reclaimed land were as alluring as those in the Indies—and he was hired to supervise many of these new ventures. Between 1600 and 1650, the year Leeghwater died, nearly 130,000 acres of land were reclaimed from Dutch lakes.

The work of the Dutch pioneers in attaining mastery of water led inevitably to Holland's taking on the greatest challenge of all, the draining of the Zuiderzee. From the mid-17th Century to the end of the 19th, the Dutch had improved the techniques developed by their predecessors; they widened rivers, built locks, deepened harbors and turned Amsterdam and Rotterdam into North Sea ports by digging waterways between them and the sea. They were close to striking a balance with nature, except when occasional heavy storms undid much that

had been accomplished. The Zuiderzee, however, remained: a million acres of often turbulent water mocking any notion of Holland's attaining a strong lead in the struggle.

The idea of changing the salt-water inland sea partly into land and partly into a freshwater lake had been proposed as early as 1667. Hendrik Stevin, a mathematician, suggested that this could be achieved by constructing dams across all the inlets between the northern Dutch islands and across those separating the islands from the mainland. "In this enclosing line," he wrote, "there shall be as many sluices as are sufficient for the water at ebb tide to empty into the North Sea. In that way, it is evident, the Zuiderzee can, at all times, be kept at the lowest ebb level, and (because there will never be any salt water flowing in but a continuous supply of fresh river water) it will gradually become fresh. Yes, without doubt it will yield a lot of land fit to be diked in."

STEVIN'S suggestion for connecting the northern Dutch islands and filling in much of the Waddenzee to create new polders was inherently sound, but he was some three centuries ahead of his time; because of the urgency of other work, the Dutch do not now believe they can get around to the so-called Waddenzee plan until the year 2000. When the Zuiderzee project, which called for a 20-mile-long dam between two points on the mainland, was started in 1927, it was based on the plans of Cornelis Lely. Lely was a single-minded engineer who dedicated his life to taming the Zuiderzee. His career has none of the qualities associated with that of a national hero, yet his accomplishments exceed in daring and imagination those of Holland's sea captains and explorers of the golden century.

Lely's early life had its share of disappointments. After receiving his engineering degree from Delft University, he found a job with the Ministry of Waterworks; but in 1886, when he was 32 and had not risen above the rank of low level bureaucrat, he was fired, for reasons no one now knows. Not long after that, several

WADDENZEE PLAN
Proposed dams
Proposed polders

North Sea

GRONINGEN

LEEUWARDEN

1600
1400
1280
1200
1427

WIERINGERMEER

1932

IJSSELMEER (ZUIDERZEE)

Darkened area
indicates land
which would
remain above
water if all dikes
were removed

1847
1610
1456
1599
1608
1631
1564
1683
1626
1622
1872

1930

1635
1612

1942
NORTHEAST
POLDER

1957
EAST
FLEVOLAND

UNDER CONSTRUCTION

1852

AMSTERDAM

HAARLEMMERMEER

UTRECHT

THE NETHERLANDS

THE HAGUE
ROTTERDAM

ARNHEM

DELTA PLAN
Dams under
construction

1957

RHINE R.

GERMANY

1961

1958

MIDDELBURG

WALCHEREN

SCHELDT R.

EINDHOVEN

MEUSE R.

Fresh water
Salt water

B E L G I U M

BARRIERS raised against the sea have greatly increased the area of the Netherlands since diking began 1,000 years ago, as this map indicates. If all the dikes, dams, sluices and pumps now in place were removed, the entire region shown in the lighter tint would lie under water—for if these barriers had not been erected over the centuries, the action of the sea would have submerged even areas not originally below water level. The dates scattered throughout this region denote the years in which dams were completed or in which sections were drained to create polders, or usable land. There are innumerable other polders, particularly in the southern Netherlands, besides the major ones marked here. Additional polders (shaded lines) will eventually be created in the north under the Waddenzee plan, which will link the coastal islands to the mainland. Salt water will be left in some areas to allow for the passage of ships and to facilitate drainage, as elsewhere. In other places fresh water will replace the salt. The Delta plan, due for completion in 1980, is intended primarily to provide protection against disastrous coastal floods.

businessmen formed the Zuiderzee Association to sponsor a study of the feasibility of closing the Zuiderzee, and put Lely in charge. In 1891 Lely submitted his plan to the prime minister. The plan was not accepted. On the basis of it, however, Lely was appointed Minister of Waterworks.

In a proper fairy tale, the hero returning as boss of the office from which he had once been fired would have put his plan into action and then would have been properly rewarded. The Dutch capacity for fairy tales is limited, however. Lely had to wait for his third term as minister before he felt he had enough support to push the government to act. At last, in 1913, he

heard Queen Wilhelmina tell the States-General, "I consider the time has come to undertake the enclosure and reclamation of the Zuiderzee. The result will be improved water control conditions in the adjacent provinces, extension of territory and a permanent increase in the opportunities of employment."

Engineering and tidal studies, however, took years to complete. It was not until 1917 that a bill was passed, 1925 that the first contracts were let, 1927 that the dam was started and 1932 that it was completed. Lely died in 1929. A statue of him stands at the western end of the enclosing dam, and the capital city of the 12th Dutch province which will be created behind the dam has been named, appropriately enough, Lelystad.

Lely's plan has remained the basis for work that is still going on. "It was," according to a modern hydraulics engineer, "the best plan that could ever have been chosen; even now, from year to year, it is constantly found to possess new advantages." There are, for example, the benefits from the fresh-water IJsselmeer itself. Before it was transformed, the Zuiderzee salted the land on which it bordered, seeping underground great distances and destroying the soil for farming. Not only was that problem solved, but the IJsselmeer serves as a huge reservoir during the summer when the Rhine and Meuse Rivers and rainfall together do not provide enough fresh drinking and irrigation water.

FOR a brief period after the enclosing dam was completed, however, many Dutchmen, especially those who lived on the coast of the former Zuiderzee, were convinced that the change was a curse, not a blessing. The fishermen were the first to note the difference; within a year after the dam was built there were hardly any eels to be caught. Instead, the lake and the villages on its shores were covered with a thick blanket of mosquitoes. To the deeply religious residents this was akin to the plagues of Egypt, God's revenge for tampering with His handiwork. Biblical or not, the mosquitoes were so thick that small boys gathered them into clusters and threw them at each other as if they were snowballs. The insects covered windshields and made driving impossible; windshield wipers merely crushed them into an opaque mass.

The answer, when it was shortly found, was incredibly simple. Scientists discovered that the eels, which breed in the Sargasso Sea and complete their long journey to Holland between May and September, are night travelers. But the IJsselmeer sluices were being opened only during the daytime, when the eels remained asleep in the mud outside. By merely opening the sluices at night, the Dutch reaped a fresh harvest. Millions of eels swam through, grew fat on the mosquitoes and promptly got caught by the fishermen, who grew fat on their increased profits.

Further benefits from Lely's plan have already been realized to some extent, but most are still in the future. Wieringermeer, the first polder reclaimed in the IJsselmeer, now houses 8,000 people on prosperous farmland. As it grew to its present size, it served as a laboratory for both scientific and sociological testing. Extensive experiments were carried out on the soil, and various crops were grown to determine the best way to use the new land. This was not too difficult; the Dutch had worked on the problems of cultivating crops on reclaimed land for years. Wieringermeer as a social laboratory was something else. The number of people, the size of farms, the layouts of villages, school and church needs, shops, streets and parks had to be carefully planned. The polder's development, moreover, was interrupted toward the end of World War II when the Nazis dynamited the Wieringermeer dike and flooded the area, an act of no strategic value whatsoever. For six months the land lay under water. Fortunately, since the enclosing dam was not affected, it was fresh water. Crops were raised within a year after the area had been redrained, although it took nearly nine years to reconstruct buildings which had been destroyed by the flooding.

THE Northeast polder, which followed the Wieringermeer and is the largest up to now, is an even better example of how the Dutch have tamed the nature they inherited. Consider the area in 1942, the year it was finally pumped dry, as a rough hexagon of 119,000 acres, unpopulated except for a village which had been the island of Urk before it was incorporated into the larger land mass.

During the war little was done about populating the land, but soil testing, planning and, of course, pumping were carried on. Earlier, the location and capacity of pumping stations had been established (there are now three with eight pumps capable of discharging 120,000 gallons or more a minute), and canals had been planned. The use of the land had also been determined

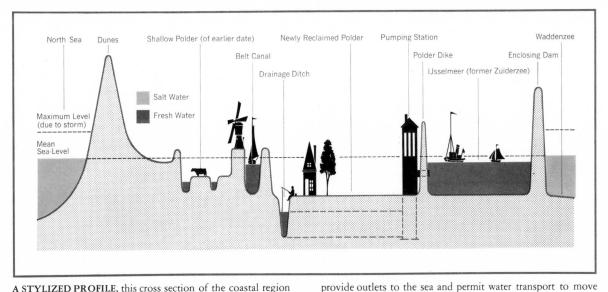

Labels on diagram:

North Sea · Dunes · Shallow Polder (of earlier date) · Newly Reclaimed Polder · Pumping Station · Waddenzee

Belt Canal · Polder Dike · Enclosing Dam

Drainage Ditch · IJsselmeer (former Zuiderzee)

Salt Water
Fresh Water

Maximum Level (due to storm)

Mean Sea-Level

A STYLIZED PROFILE, this cross section of the coastal region of the Netherlands illustrates some of the techniques used by the Dutch to maintain their land below sea level. At left dunes have been raised far above the highest known rise of the North Sea. Small canals crossing the early polder carry the water which continually seeps inland to the belt canal. Belt canals provide outlets to the sea and permit water transport to move far inland. The polder at center consists of land reclaimed from the former Zuiderzee, drained and kept dry by power pumping stations which send excess water into the IJsselmeer, a freshwater lake created from the Zuiderzee when the enclosing dam at far right was raised against the Waddenzee in 1932.

(it had proved to be deficient in nitrogen, requiring the early cultivation of crops to enrich the soil), and plans had also been made for the disposition of archeological finds (mammoths and other animals from the ice ages, tools from the Stone Age and 160 wrecked ships are now in a museum in the polder).

The Northeast polder was in fact ready for settlement barely in time to meet a new emergency brought on by the end of the war. In 1944, the Allies had bombed the dikes of the island of Walcheren, which was held by the Germans to control the approaches to Antwerp. Four large breaches were made, and the salt water poured over 40,000 acres. By the time the Walcheren dikes were closed again late in 1945 and the salt water had been drained off the land, the government had decided that the time had come to effect some basic land reforms throughout the area. For the most part, this consisted of bringing together two or more small farms to create a large, more efficient farm. Under ordinary circumstances this would have left a number of farmers farmless. But with the new land in the Northeast polder, the problem was solved. First choice of land was given to the so-called "pioneers," those who had worked on the polder during the Nazi occupation; but second choice went to those who had been dispossessed by either the flood or land reform on Walcheren.

Generally speaking, the Dutch have sought to establish a representation from each of the provinces in the new polder. This has been managed in part. They have also, of course, sought a balanced religious division, but with less success. One of the interesting social phenomena uncovered by this project is that Protestants are more willing to emigrate from their birthplaces than are Catholics.

The Dutch have however succeeded in establishing a balanced agricultural economy in the new polder. Variation in types of farming is encouraged—there are nearly 300 dairy farms, more than 100 truck farms and about 60 fruit farms. Some 1,600 separate farms have been set up; the government retains some for experimental work, and the rest are rented on long term leases at very low rates.

To serve the farmers, 10 villages and one fair-sized town, Emmeloord, have been built. The villages vary in population from 500 to 1,200; Emmeloord has more than 7,000 people and is expected to house 10,000 in a few years. New as Emmeloord and the villages are, they are already acquiring distinct personalities. Even an uninspired sameness in building design—brick and glass predominate—has not completely destroyed local initiative. Architectural variations do appear, especially in the churches, whose bell towers are usually the tallest structures in each town.

The lessons learned on the Northeast polder—from diking techniques to town planning—will be applied to Eastern Flevoland, the third of the five planned IJsselmeer polders. Eastern Flevoland is already dry, and Lelystad, which is projected as a city of at least 30,000, already exists, although as no more than a shack town for the polder workers. Before Lelystad attains its full growth or Eastern Flevoland is fully cultivated, Southern Flevoland and Markerwaard will be started. Dutch planners now lean toward developing the last two as suburban and industrial polders, rather than as farming areas—an unprecedented move. The growth of industry in the country, especially around Amsterdam, makes this a logical departure.

AS if completing Cornelis Lely's plans by 1978 were not enough of a national job, the Dutch have been forced to take on another mammoth project, one even tougher than the reclamation of the Zuiderzee. Known as the Delta plan, it calls for massive dams to be built between the islands of the southwestern province of Zeeland. These islands are the ones that were so terribly battered during the 1953 storm in which giant waves whipped on by 100- to 115-mile-an-hour winds tore through the dikes. Before the crisis was over, 1,800 men, women and children had died, and 70,000 people had to be evacuated from the area. Sixty-seven major breaks and more than 500 minor ones were ripped into the southwest dikes, and 375,000 acres of farmland—4.5 per cent of Holland's land area—were flooded with salt water. Ironically, the blow came just five days after the Dutch government had informed the United States that it no longer required Marshall Plan assistance. The country had attained the "viability" that had been set as the purpose and goal of American help to the nations of Europe.

Holland gave immediate proof of its viability.

The 67th major gap in the dike was closed on November 6, 1953, nine months and five days after the storm had struck, and just before the beginning of the new winter storm season. "The dikes are closed," Queen Juliana told an anxiously waiting nation. "The end of the flood disaster situation is in sight. We may expect that soon our territory will be reclaimed. . . . Then we shall have reached the stage of reconstruction of all parts of the flood area, and the building of a new future for those who will live there."

THE new future was under way even as the dikes were being repaired. Three weeks after the storm, the government had established the Delta Committee with instructions to come up with a plan to prevent similar disasters. The Delta plan goes far past pure defense against the sea. The lakes formed behind the huge barriers will become a major source of fresh water for farmers in the region; highways along the tops of the dams will bring the islands—or, more accurately, former islands by then—closer to the rest of the country.

The present village way of life there will probably die because of the expected influx of people to the currently sparsely settled region. Recreation facilities on the new lakes will bring tourists from within Holland as well as from abroad. Industry is a good possibility, too, because the islands are close to burgeoning Rotterdam. New ways of earning a living will necessarily have to be introduced. Among the casualties of the Delta plan will be the oyster fishermen who work the famous Zeeland oyster beds. With the new sea walls in place, the oysters will disappear, a decided loss to gastronomy as well as to the local economy.

Objections have been heard, as they were along the coasts of the former Zuiderzee, that the end of local traditions is too high a price to pay for an uncertain future, however rosily it is painted. But the objections are not likely to prevail in the face of the far older tradition of keeping Holland's head above water.

A modern dike, studded with tough basalt blocks, provides a low-tide promenade (left) as it shields the Netherlands from the sea.

The Never-ending Battle with the Besieging Sea

The Dutch have fought for centuries to fend off the battering of the sea and to control flood-prone rivers. Slowly, with infinite effort and many reverses, they have linked together an amazing 2,000-mile-long system of dunes and dikes. Without these, 40 per cent of the area of the Netherlands would be under water, including the chief cities and ports. Characteristic of the Dutch was their energetic reaction to the terrible flood of 1953. Within 10 months they had closed the 67 large holes the North Sea had punched in their dikes. But, not content with repairs, they resolved to throw a new series of enclosing dams across the sea gaps in the Delta area southwest of Rotterdam. When the Delta plan is completed in 1980, the Dutch will have taken another step in converting their ancient enemy into their friend.

STREET OF WATER is formed by a branch of the Rhine in Katwijk, Holland. Navigable by light craft like the barge in the distance, the river almost washes the doorsteps of the houses on its banks. Every house has its wharf and the townspeople use the river virtually as a village street. The Katwijk area is protected from the sea by locks built in 1804-1807.

COZY FARMHOUSE is embedded in the outer slope of a dike (*above*) on the Rhine. Like most Dutch dikes, this one has a roadway on top. The house is below the river's water level.

CAREFUL FARMER forks weed and grass into his rowboat (*opposite*) beside one of the drainage ditches that help keep the surrounding polder—reclaimed land—from being flooded.

INGENIOUS USES are made of the ubiquitous water and the dikes that control it

SHATTERED DIKES allow the North Sea *(lower left)* to pour across the low-lying island of Schouwen-Duiveland in the estuary of the East Scheldt. Some 1,800 people died in the floods.

JUMBLED WRECKAGE drifts against the houses of a flooded inland town *(opposite)*. The 1953 floods, the worst in a century, covered 375,000 acres and destroyed or damaged 47,000 houses.

IMMENSE DAMS *take shape as the Dutch*
prepare new defenses against the sea

CLOSING A GAP, tugboats inch a last caisson into position as the dam across the Veerse Gat is completed in 1961. This was the first major closing of a sea gap under the Delta plan.

PREPARING A BARRICADE, engineers build huge sluices in a dam to close the Haringvliet gap *(right)*. The sluices will allow winter ice from the Rhine and Meuse to flow into the sea.

A sunny parlor, with a bright tile floor and pots of flowers, is the gathering place of the Gridelet family on a Sunday morning before the

men go out hunting. Their home is in Belgium's Ardennes region.

Pride and Provincialism

THE deep-seated provincialism which pervades the Low Countries was once satirized by the brilliant Belgian writer Michel de Ghelderode. He described the arrival of Kwiebe-Kwiebus, a mythical Flemish philosopher, in a city "divided into one hundred very well delimited districts, each one having its belfry with its bell. Kwiebus went from district to district, noticing that the inhabitants of one district had no desire to know the inhabitants of the other." In each he met idlers who exclaimed, "Isn't our bell unique; could there possibly exist another that even approaches it in accuracy, tone, size, form, the peal of its tongue?"

Kwiebus then moved to the adjacent district, "where people pursued him with the same remarks. Having scoured the town in this way and heard one hundred different bells, Kwiebus concluded that these connoisseurs . . . by dint of hearing only one bell, heard only one sound."

The inability to hear bells other than their own is characteristic of Dutchmen as well as of

Belgians. One obvious reason for this is the essentially small-town nature of the Low Countries. Only 14 cities in the Netherlands and five in Belgium have populations which exceed 100,000. Of these, only Amsterdam, Rotterdam, The Hague, Brussels and Antwerp have more than half a million people; no city in the Low Countries has a million. Some two thirds of the Dutch population is scattered among 968 communities, of which 533 have fewer than 5,000 people each. Belgium is even more fragmented; it has 2,633 communes—autonomous local governments—of which 1,733 have fewer than 2,000 people. Among them is Zoutenaaie, with a total of 25 citizens from five families. Because of a law which forbids more than one member of a family to sit on a commune council, Zoutenaaie has to import two inhabitants from a neighboring commune to bring its council to full strength.

COMPOUNDING the divisions within their society are the more than 15,000 social and professional organizations created by the Belgians. These groups are often important politically as well as socially, although some of them have no nobler purpose than the consumption of beer. The names of the societies indicate or cloak their purposes, depending on the mood of the group at the time of decision. Cercle de l'Avenir de l'Ecole 13 (Association for the Advancement of School Number 13) would be recognized by any American P.T.A. member, while l'Espoir du Centre (The Hope of the Center) could be anything from a drinking club to a political debating society. De Pottenzuipers van bij Patje (The Old Soaks from Patty's Café), Les Joyeux Joueurs de Balle (The Happy Ball Players), l'Harmonie Philanthropique Franco-Belge (The Franco-Belgian Philanthropic Music Club) are more or less self-explanatory, as is one that may well be the most exclusive of all—Association des Fabricants de Poignées de Marteaux de Bas-Ixelles (Association of Hammer-Handle Makers of Lower Ixelles).

Voluntary associations aside, provincialism in the Low Countries is intensified by language

divisions beyond the basic French-Dutch split in Belgium. Within the confined area of the Low Countries, five distinct languages are spoken—Dutch by 17 million people, French by four million, German (in the border towns) by 60,000, Luxembourgeois by 315,000 and Frisian by 480,000.

DUTCH, like English, is a Germanic language. Despite the common origins, however, Germans find it difficult to speak Dutch without a strong accent. During World War II, in fact, Dutch patriots could always detect Germans in civilian clothes with a simple test— the pronunciation of Scheveningen, the name of the North Sea resort outside The Hague. To a Dutchman it is simple to pronounce the first three letters as if they were two distinct sounds, the "s" followed by a gentle guttural for the "ch." A German invariably runs the letters together as if they were the "sh" in shell. Prince Bernhard is usually cited as a German who comes close to achieving accentless Dutch, but the Prince's triumph is far from complete; parlor comics in the Netherlands mimic Bernhard's speech in much the same way that their American counterparts mimic President Kennedy's Boston accent.

Although all Dutchmen speak Dutch, local and regional dialects rooted in tradition have not disappeared with increased travel or the influence of radio and television. A resident of the northern Dutch province of Groningen, for example, has difficulty being understood in Utrecht, in the center of the country, unless he uses the formal, school-taught Dutch—the city hall language, as some call it. In the Dutch-speaking area of Belgium, local variations are so strongly entrenched that people in neighboring towns are sometimes more bewildered than enlightened by each other.

Except for occasional differences in phraseology, written Dutch is almost exactly the same throughout the Netherlands and Flemish Belgium. Books written by Flemish authors, which sell better in Holland than they do in Belgium, are no more difficult for a Dutchman to comprehend than a book written by an American is for an Englishman. A Fleming writes of someone who rises from a chair, for example, that *"Hij staat recht,"* which is literally translated as "He stands straight." A Dutchman, on the other hand, writes it as *"Hij staat op,"* which is translated as "He stands up." No literate Dutchman objects to such phrasings; rather, he cherishes them for the Flemish flavor they add to an author's style.

The Netherlands is not normally considered a bilingual country, and for all practical purposes it is not. Nevertheless, Frisian, which is limited to the province of Friesland, is recognized by linguists as a language rather than a dialect. Like Dutch, it is related to Low German, but it developed along different paths and the language is, if anything, closer to English. Frisians, on the other hand, also read, write and speak Dutch. They do insist, however, on teaching Frisian in their schools in order to keep alive their cultural heritage. During World War II the Nazis tried to encourage a Frisian nationalism in an effort to separate the province from the rest of Holland, but they found very few takers.

B ELGIAN French is undeniably French, both written and spoken, but guidebooks to Belgium published in France usually find it necessary to alert their readers to certain idiosyncrasies. The Belgians do not employ the same names for numbers that the French do. They say *septante* instead of *soixante-dix* for seventy and *nonante* instead of the cumbersome *quatre-vingt-dix* for ninety. A host of colloquialisms also keep Belgian French at a small remove from French French. Belgians use the word *athénée* instead of *lycée* to identify any state high school, and *lycée* only when they mean a girls' high school. Belgians seek to elicit a reaction to a meal by asking *"Ça goûte?"* (Does it taste?). A Frenchman desiring the same information asks *"Ça vous plaît?"* (Does it please you?).

Belgium has still another tongue, known as Walloon. It is basically a Romance dialect—

part of the group from which modern French descends—and is used by some three million persons in the Walloon provinces. In the Middle Ages a number of works were produced in Walloon. Even though central authorities attempted to suppress its use, it enjoyed a revival in the 17th Century, chiefly in plays and comic operas. In 1856 the Société Liégoise de Littérature Wallonne was founded to keep the dialect and its literature alive. Today, country weeklies are printed in Walloon, and a Walloon dramatic society produces the old plays. The Belgian government has encouraged the literary movement, but in view of the problems Belgium already has with both Dutch and French, no one has seriously suggested that Walloon be officially recognized. Luxembourgers also have two languages. French is the official one, but for home use and patriotic expression the Luxembourgers employ a dialect known as Luxembourgeois, which is basically German with a large admixture of French.

The variety of languages and dialects, the seemingly disproportionate number of tiny, autonomous communities, the political and religious splits and the thousands of separate organizations they have spawned are likely to be integral parts of the Low Countries for years to come. The provincialism which has resulted is reflected at its best in the charm of old customs maintained, traditional clothes and the pageantry of folk festivals. At its worst it has led to bigotry, smugness, a refusal to seek new answers to old problems and a profound and divisive jealousy between groups.

I F there is any hope for change it may become apparent with the coming of age of the postwar generation. Its members are among the most avid readers of the young writers who have made provincialism one of their major targets (see Chapter 6). The job of closing the old rifts will not be an easy one, though. In Belgium, one is almost forced to take sides in the Flemish-Walloon controversy. In Holland, the splits are being intensified by the rapid increase in the country's population.

Jean-Baptiste Clamance, the narrator in Albert Camus' last novel, *The Fall,* looked at Holland as "this crowd of people swarming on the pavements, wedged into a little space of houses and canals, hemmed in by fog, cold lands, and the sea steaming like wet washing." The Netherlands Central Bureau of Statistics evokes the same image with less artistry but more specifics. The official government figures show that the population of Holland is growing at a faster annual rate than that of any other country in Western Europe. The population has more than doubled so far in the 20th Century, and if the rate of growth remains the same, as seems likely, the present 12 million people will become 18 to 20 million before the beginning of the 21st Century. The Dutch have the world's longest life expectancy—71 years for men, 73.9 for women—and the world's lowest death rate—7.5 per thousand.

In all but a few of the other Western European countries such a population boom would be considered a blessing; in Holland's narrow space it is a problem with no apparent solution. Stranger still, while editors, politicians and businessmen consider overpopulation a distinct menace, there is hardly any public discussion of the subject.

THE reluctance openly to meet an issue with important social, economic and political consequences may be uncharacteristic of people who pride themselves on their foresight on such matters as flood control and land reclamation. However, it is characteristic of the Dutch—sharply split as they are along religious lines—to avoid a controversy which, in its initial stages at least, could only intensify the division. A debate on population would necessarily cover birth control and contraception, family allowances and even premarital sex relations (because an ever-present housing shortage is a major cause for postponement of marriages among the young). And these are precisely the subjects on which Protestants,

Catholics and humanists (by Dutch terminology, non-church members) can become their most emotional.

The Catholic position is that the problem is of no immediate importance, that population increases slow down as often as they speed up. The case of Belgium is often cited to support this contention. Until it was surpassed by Holland soon after World War II, Belgium contained more people per square mile than any country in the world; since then Belgium's rate of growth has decreased to a steady .5 per cent per year, and overpopulation is not a problem. Except for a small group among them which feels that contraceptives "should be available to all those who consider their use allowable," Catholics oppose government sponsorship of birth-control information, as they do elsewhere. Protestants find this view inconsistent with Catholic insistence that government family allowances be continued at their present rate. Both Protestants and humanists feel that Holland's population problem could be controlled by decreasing government allowances for children.

The Dutch government prefers to make do with patchwork solutions—a tacit admission that the problem exists, of course—but the patches have not been completely effective. After World War II, emigration was encouraged. Prince Bernhard became an unofficial employment agent abroad, extolling the virtues of Dutch farmers and laborers. Many Dutchmen, eager to break out of the confinement of Holland or fearing another war, did leave for Canada, Australia, New Zealand and the United States.

BY the end of 1962, about 900,000 Dutchmen had left the Netherlands, but the annual departures have fallen from a postwar high of 75,000 in 1952 to fewer than 40,000 in 1961 and 1962. The Dutch government anticipates that the new polders being completed in the IJsselmeer will relieve some of the pressure from the intensely populated industrial areas around Amsterdam. Some officials have suggested that present provisions for recreation areas may have to be sharply curtailed. Others believe that when the countries of the Common Market are fully integrated, many Dutchmen will gravitate elsewhere in search of living space.

There is no real belief, however, that any of these proposals, or all of them together, will really solve the problem. The results of overpopulation may not reach the crisis stage for many years, but a crisis is patently inevitable.

The most serious current problem directly attributable to the population increase is housing. Holland came out of the war with 85,000 dwellings totally destroyed and hundreds of thousands partially damaged. By the time the money and materials were available to begin to fill this shortage, additional families and children were clamoring for even more housing. Strict regulations were laid down for occupancy of apartments and houses, and tight rent controls were established. Doubling up came to be considered normal, and the one-family house a luxury enjoyed mainly by foreigners.

ALTHOUGH older people are the only ones who can remember when housing was not tight, the Dutch in their steady, plodding way have been dealing with this particular problem. Some 85,000 new houses are being built each year. This is not enough, however, and rents have gone up, reflecting increased costs. To keep construction moving in an orderly fashion, government controls are still involved in nearly every aspect of housing—location, rents and architecture.

It is in the cities, of course, that the overcrowding is most noticeable, and the continued exodus of young people from country to town aggravates the situation. In Belgium there is a choice of Brussels, Antwerp or Liège. In practice most of the young people move to Brussels. Here, too, provincialism exists—the city is actually made up of 18 different communes—but this is hardly noticeable to a new resident. Brussels is a busy and cosmopolitan city, overcrowded and choking on its own

THE VIGOR OF TRADITIONAL RITUALS

Although religious and cultural differences originating far back in history still engender bitter rivalry and occasional violence in the Low Countries, these same ancient beliefs and customs also produce a wealth of engaging festivals and rituals. A sampling of these feast days and other observances follows.

VASTENAVOND, or Fast Eve, is the final event of the Dutch pre-Lenten festival. In southern Holland, the merrymaking lasts three days. Preparations for the carnival are made on the eleventh day of the eleventh month (November 11) by a council of 11 citizens, since 11 is the number traditionally associated with fools, and the carnival invites all sorts of foolish behavior.

PAASZONDAG, Easter Sunday, is celebrated with bonfires in the eastern Dutch provinces. Every household must contribute its share of wood to the fire, and neighborhoods vie to produce the most glorious blaze. After the bonfires are well started, the people join hands and dance about them singing hymns.

SINT NICOLAAS AVOND, or the Eve of Saint Nicholas, is celebrated in Holland on the 5th of December. In the 11th Century, Nicholas, a Near Eastern saint, became the guardian of sailors. By the 13th Century, seagoing Dutchmen had built 23 churches in his honor. In the 14th Century, the saint became associated with children and gift-giving when the choir boys of Holland's many Saint Nicholas churches began parading through the streets begging for "bishop money" on December 6, the supposed birthday of the saint. In time, convent schools took up the holiday. A monk would dress up in long, white beard and red cloak and reward good students with gifts. It soon came to be believed that the saint, assisted by Black Peter, the devil (chained for the day by the saint), rode over the town rooftops and dropped candy and gifts down the chimneys. The Dutch settlers of course brought their Saint Nicholas (nicknamed Sinterklaas) to America. Later he merged with the merry, Falstaffian Father Christmas brought by English settlers, but his name became Santa Claus, an Anglicized version of his Dutch nickname. The Dutch celebrations are still elaborate, especially in Amsterdam where Saint Nicholas and Black Peter arrive by boat, parade through the streets and are received by the queen.

THE PROCESSION OF THE HOLY BLOOD in Bruges originated in 1150 when the knight Thierry d'Alsace returned from the Second Crusade bringing a phial said to contain a drop of Christ's blood. This relic, preserved in a lavish gold reliquary, is paraded through the city on the first Monday after May 2 each year.

THE MARRIAGE OF GOLIATH, which takes place in August in Ath, Belgium, is one of the most spectacular of the many Belgian parades of giants. Figures 20 feet tall, made of wicker and cloth, are carried through the streets and include Goliath with helmet and breastplate, his bride with orange blossoms in her hair, Samson and a fierce-looking warrior named Ambiorix.

traffic as are most big cities of the world, but it still has its charms. Its Grand' Place is probably the most beautiful public square in Europe; the gilded baroque facades, restrained by day in the gray natural light, shine brilliantly under the floodlights aimed at them at night.

The cafés in the Grand' Place are invariably crowded with Bruxellois as well as tourists. The square has been a popular meeting place since the Middle Ages. Brussels' reputation for gaiety probably started then, too, and despite the many occupations of the city by foreign powers, it has managed to keep the reputation. For the ambitious, Brussels is the focal point of Belgian power. It is not only the seat of government; it contains banks, the home offices of the businesses which run the country, and the administrative headquarters of the Common Market and Euratom. The city combines the features of Washington and New York, and has been often compared to Paris. Its personality, bilingualism included, is nevertheless its own.

Although the Dutch States-General meets in The Hague and the foreign embassies are located there, and while the major shipping companies and many of the country's new industries are in Rotterdam, Amsterdam is still Holland's most important city. It is not only the financial but the intellectual center as well. The Hague is considered by all but its residents (and sometimes even by them too) as the biggest village in Europe; Rotterdam may be bustling and modern, but Amsterdam has held a special place for the Dutch ever since the wealthy burghers of the 17th Century built their beautiful town houses (and almost as beautiful warehouses) on its canals.

BECAUSE the sea silt and alluvial clay on which Amsterdam is situated cannot support heavy structures, contractors have had to drive wooden piles to more substantial earth and then build the houses on the piles. The ancient piles, nicknamed *juffers*, or young ladies, still support old Amsterdam, although they represent problems for modern engineers.

The water level around Amsterdam must be maintained high enough to cover the piles completely because exposure to the air would cause them to rot. But the water cannot be permitted to rise too high or it would run over the sides of the canals and flood the cellars. If either of these eventualities occurred, Amsterdam's stately homes would be in danger of collapse. The possibility of that catastrophe inspired a jingle many years ago, which is still sung by Dutch schoolchildren:

> *Amsterdam, die grote stad,*
> *Die is gebouwd op palen.*
> *En als-ie dan eens ommevalt*
> *Wie zal dat dan betalen?*
>
> *Amsterdam, that great town,*
> *Is built on piles.*
> *If one day it topples down*
> *Who will pay the bills?*

Amsterdam's collapse being generally considered unlikely, the city is still the primary goal for Dutch youngsters. It has two universities—the Municipal University with 7,000 students, the country's largest, and the Free (Calvinist) University with 2,000. Many ambitious students tend to remain in Amsterdam after graduation. Those with artistic pretensions find inspiration in the bars and coffeehouses around the Leidseplein, Amsterdam's version of Greenwich Village and Saint Germain-des-Prés. The nation's major newspapers and publishing houses are in Amsterdam and so were, at last count, 49 of the nation's 427 museums and private collections currently open to the public.

Neither Amsterdam nor Brussels is representative of Holland or Belgium, although each has its quota of the petty provincialism which rules the rest of the Low Countries. But as sophisticated cities, they have less of it. Conceivably, given time and enough young people who see no merit in constant bickering, Amsterdam and Brussels can show Holland and Belgium the way to break through the confines of provincialism.

Vacationers relax in a café at Scheveningen, Holland. The resort draws many Germans, as the posted menu, in German, attests.

Ample Diversions Brightening Industrious Lives

The businesslike people of the Low Countries, even though beset by overcrowding and other problems, still approach life with considerable gaiety and spirit. They love festivals, games and especially vacations among the beauties of their gardenlike lands. When summer comes, the beach resorts, such as Scheveningen, seen above and on the next two pages, are suddenly thronged and campers invade the forests and hills. Even in the dour winters, there is evidence everywhere that the people round out their energetic lives with laughter and song.

FAMILY GROUP sits amidst a pleasant disorder of beach para-
phernalia at Scheveningen, a Dutch resort. The breezes are often
sharp even in the summer, requiring windscreens and sweaters.

TEEN-AGE GIRLS in bikinis *(below)* bask in the lee of two of
Scheveningen's peanut-shell-shaped wicker beach chairs. Scheveningen has been a fixture of Dutch life for over a century.

AMUSEMENT PIER juts 1,200 feet into the sea *(above)* from the Scheveningen promenade. This new pier, with its 140-foot-high tower, replaced one which burned during World War II.

MASSED CHAIRS cover a section of Scheveningen's beach *(left)*. The promenade and its hotels *(background)* are built on top of a massive dike which stretches 20 miles up the coast.

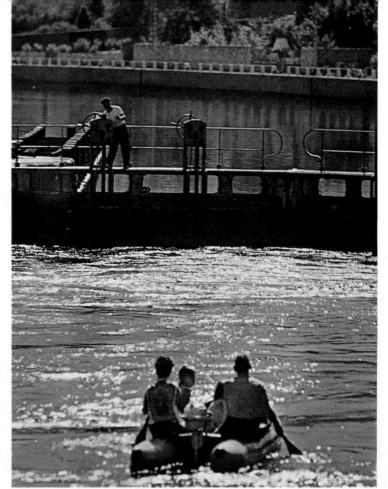

DOUGHTY NAVIGATORS paddle a pontoon craft toward a lock on the Meuse near Dinant. Locks help stabilize the water's depth, making the river navigable through most of its length.

MOTORIZED BARGES, one lashed to flatboats full of coal, ride at anchor *(left)* near an old, neat Meuse Valley town. The bargeman's family stands on the deck of the more distant barge.

GREEN CAMPSITE offers a pleasant stop *(below)* for trailers near Bouvignes on the Meuse. Although the Meuse flows past several industrial centers, much of its valley is calmly pastoral.

MOTORSCOOTER RALLY brings club members in white coveralls and crash helmets roaring into Namur during a Sunday cross-country run. Belgians are especially fond of clubs, sports and competitions.

PATIENT FISHERMEN cast from the bank of the Moselle *(opposite)* near Remich, Luxembourg, standing on fill which is part of a project to deepen the river. Luxembourg has many fine trout streams.

SUNNY AFTERNOON affords the people of Tournai a chance to play *boules* *(right)*, a form of lawn bowling popular in Europe. The crouching man is measuring to see who got his ball nearest the target.

MODEST CAFES serve as cheerful clubhouses where neighborhood people can meet friends and play games

INFORMAL DANCE to the music of a jukebox amuses some young couples in Antwerp during a sunny weekend afternoon. Belgian teenagers are fond of American jazz and rock and roll.

CHESS CLUB in Antwerp meets weekly in a café *(above)*. The clocks are for timing the moves, each player being required to make a certain number of moves within a set period of time.

ACCORDION PLAYER whiles away a Sunday afternoon *(opposite)* amusing a Belgian family and an onlooker in a Brussels café. A great many Belgians are eager amateur musicians.

DECORATIVE BALLOONS are hung in a Namur café *(right)* by a waitress in preparation for a local celebration. The Belgian calendar abounds in carnival days and religious festivals.

CONCERTGOERS animatedly discuss a performance by Amsterdam's famous Concertgebouw orchestra in the lobby of the concert hall *(above)*. The orchestra was founded in 1888.

AUDIENCE almost surrounds the musicians in the Concertgebouw hall *(below)*, even filling the area behind the orchestra *(foreground)*. The orchestra has toured Europe and the U.S.

WINE FESTIVAL in Grevenmacher, Luxembourg *(above)*, is led by a rotund "Festival King" who prepares to drain his goblet. Grevenmacher is a winegrowing village on the Moselle.

TRADITIONAL DANCERS in costumes of the Moselle River Valley *(below)* move through a folk dance during the Grevenmacher wine festival, which is held the last part of September.

Leading "Eurocrats" converse around cluttered tables as a meeting of the Commission of the Common Market adjourns. The commission,

established in Brussels, drafts plans for increasing European unity.

9

The Vanishing Customs House

IN the muddy autumn of 1944, the end of the war in the Low Countries lay in sight. The last counterattack of the Germans was yet to come. But by September 5, Antwerp and Brussels had been liberated, and Allied forces stood poised for the final thrust into Holland and Luxembourg. On that same day in London the representatives in exile of Belgium, the Netherlands and Luxembourg solemnly signed a document entitled, somewhat austerely, Customs Convention. Unlike a number of other proposals and public statements by Allied officials issued that optimistic last fall of the war, the Customs Convention of the Benelux nations—a word formed from the initial letters of the three countries' names—had no high-flown phrases about a brave new world a-borning.

In keeping with the commercial tradition of the Low Countries, it was a thoroughly businesslike paper. Its preamble consisted of a simple declaration that the governments of the three countries, "desiring, at the moment of the liberation . . . to create the most favorable conditions for the ultimate formation of a complete and durable economic union and for the restoration of economic activity, have decided to further these ends by establishing a common tariff of import duties."

THE articles which ensued might have made interesting reading in a college economics classroom, but they would not necessarily have stirred resistance fighters to action. Words like levies, rates, duties, adjustments, disputes, licenses, transit quotas and administrative charges were sprinkled liberally through the convention's nine brief clauses. Yet behind the heavy prose lay an adventurous project—a voluntary economic integration of sovereign nations. Years of negotiation remained before major steps toward the goal could be taken. But the bold idea of economic integration eventually led to other plans for postwar unions that were ultimately to be no less than revolutionary in their impact on world events.

It would be pleasant, but completely inaccurate, to report that after the Low Countries were liberated they immediately ratified the convention, achieved the goal of total economic union envisaged by its preamble and lived happily and wealthily ever after. Instead, traditional rivalries and jealousies which had vanished in the pain of wartime rapidly revived. The equality of the vanquished which existed at the time of the signing of the convention quickly changed after liberation as Belgium and Luxembourg discovered that they were relatively prosperous and Holland was a dismally poor relative. The idea of a Benelux economic union did not die, but neither did it seem to retain the vigor that it had possessed in preliberation days. It took until early 1948 for the Customs Convention to become operational, and it was not until 1958, and the ratification of intermediate agreements, that a Treaty of Economic Union among the three countries was signed. The treaty, which went into effect in 1960, has not yet brought a complete economic union, but no one can deny that one is on the way.

Americans used to a federal union with no customs barriers between states find that the idea of regional associations in Europe represents the highest economic logic. Europeans, with strong national traditions, have not always been convinced. After the industrial revolution, private arrangements between manufacturers from different countries were common enough, but economic arrangements between governments were somehow considered improper. Alliances were made for military emergencies or to maintain a balance of power, and integration in economic matters was achieved only by military conquest. National governments had as one of their primary goals the protection of their own farmers, merchants or manufacturers from foreign competition.

YET many Europeans had long sensed that a large, free market would make sense for Europe if the national barriers could be broken. As early as 1776, the Scottish economist and great advocate of free trade, Adam Smith, had attacked protectionist policies, writing in *The Wealth of Nations* that the productive efficiency derived from the "division," or specialization, of labor was "limited by the extent of the market."

The crossing of national boundaries by the railroads was another convincing argument, and on a limited basis certain consolidations began to take place. In 1834 a group of German principalities formed the Zollverein, or customs union. A customs union is one in which governments agree to abolish tariffs on goods produced by member countries. The Zollverein was thus a common market on what now seems a small scale. In 1842 Luxembourg, which needed a sure market for its products, joined the Zollverein. Luxembourg got its first railroad in 1859, an event of such importance that the poem "Feierwôn," written to commemorate the event, now ranks with the duchy's national anthem, "Our Homeland." When Luxembourg later attained efficient steel production and farming methods, the country's prosperity was assured; it had the products, the transportation and the Zollverein to sell within as a market.

The moral was so obvious that when the Luxembourg-Germany customs union died after the German occupation of Luxembourg in World War I, the duchy cast about for a new partner. Luxembourgers hoped to join France; the country's farmers wanted to be included in France's high protection policy on agricultural products and its businessmen liked the size of France as a market. But the French bowed out, and in 1922 the Luxembourgers formed an economic union with Belgium. Known as BLEU, the Belgium-Luxembourg Economic Union was still in existence when World War II started and had proved so beneficial to both partners that it inspired the talks which led to the Benelux Customs Convention.

The obstacles which prevented the swift consummation of the economic union of the three countries after the war were rooted in their histories. Belgium had been a manufacturing nation since the Middle Ages, when its textile mills were the most important in Europe. By the 13th Century, coal was available in the Charleroi region, and Liège had become a center for the manufacture of glass and armaments.

BY the 19th Century, Liège was the arms center of Europe, and Belgian blast furnaces were operating full time. After independence was won from Holland in 1830, an even bigger boom got under way, and with support from Leopold I banks like the Société Générale, which today is one of the world's largest holding companies, became stronger and were able to add increased support to new ventures. Long before the world was concerned with underdeveloped countries, Belgian men and money were building transportation systems, bridges, power plants and blast furnaces in countries which had never known these benefits of industrialization. At home agriculture prospered, although Belgium never managed to produce enough food for its own needs.

World War I and German occupation were disasters for the Belgian economy. In 1922 Belgium needed a good deal more than economic union with Luxembourg although that, at least, represented a start toward regaining some of its past strength.

The Dutch had developed along economic lines different from those of the Belgians. Commerce and farming had been the mainstays of the Dutch economy since the Middle Ages. Holland possessed a small textile industry, but not of a size to cause the Belgians any concern. During its fight with Spain, Protestant Holland had great appeal for non-Catholic Belgians. Diamond cutters moved north, for example, and Amsterdam became the world's diamond center (in recent years the industry has returned to Belgium). Beyond that, the Dutch carved a unique place in the maritime field. Their shipyards were the busiest in the world. One estimate is that in the mid-17th Century, some 20,000 Dutch-built ships were in service around the world, carrying crews totaling a quarter of a million men. The Dutch also led the world in the carrying trade, and their fishing industry ranked even higher on the basis of money brought in. The Dutch were as fortunate with their limited land. Dutch cheese and butter were synonyms for quality dairy products, and cows from the provinces of Friesland and Holland were highly sought.

Toward the end of the 19th Century, Holland began to industrialize. Coal mining was developed in the southern province of Limburg. Neutralism in World War I was economically beneficial, and after the war the Dutch began to increase their industrial output with new steel, electrical equipment, chemical and rayon plants. Their economy became increasingly competitive with Belgium's.

WHEN the representatives of Belgium, Luxembourg and Holland sat down during World War II to negotiate the Customs Convention, they may have hoped longingly for the simple situation which existed before World War I when the economies of Belgium and Luxembourg so nicely complemented that of the Dutch. A union then of a group of manufacturers on one side and one of shippers and farmers on the other conceivably could have been accomplished with a minimum of difficulties and negotiation.

If the prospects for union looked hopeless the negotiators for the three countries tried not to indicate it in public statements. Even after 1948, when the Customs Convention went into effect, free movement of goods, money and labor among the three countries remained a goal to be achieved. There were still too many problems. Dutch farmers produced crops more cheaply than the farmers of Belgium and Luxembourg, and lengthy and frequent conferences had to be held to work out mutually agreeable rules, some of which are still not satisfactory.

THEN came an ironic turnabout. When the reconstructed Dutch factories started producing in earnest they were easily more efficient than those of the Belgians, who, in the flush of their own postwar prosperity, had neglected to modernize their plants. The Netherlands, quite naturally, took advantage of earlier agreements and stepped up its exports to Belgium and Luxembourg. Manufacturers in those countries complained loudly, and it would not have surprised those close to the situation at the time if Benelux had quietly collapsed.

Benelux was saved primarily by the leaders in all three countries, who never abandoned the conviction that the idea of union was essentially sound. But it was also saved by the stirring of a belief in Europe that an even larger and more ambitious union was not only desirable but necessary. Holland, Belgium and Luxembourg, small countries which traditionally had to depend on the good will, purchasing power and understanding of other, larger nations, were among the first to support the new development.

Early in 1948, the 16 (later 18) nations involved in the Marshall Plan program formed the Organization for European Economic Cooperation. The OEEC was a long way from the ideals of some of the wartime speeches, but within its limits the organization established

patterns for mutual economic assistance among member nations.

The big push for European economic unity, of which Benelux was still only a promise and a symbol, came from Jean Monnet, the brilliant and farsighted French planner, who preferred to remain in the background. Monnet's plan was proposed by Robert Schuman, the French foreign minister, on May 9, 1950. In what Walter Lippmann has called "the most audacious and constructive initiative since the end of the war," Schuman (on behalf of the French government) suggested the formation of a Franco-German coal and steel community which would be subject to a supranational authority independent of either government, and he invited other countries in Europe to join it. "The pooling of coal and steel production," Schuman predicted, "will immediately provide for the establishment of common bases for economic development as a first step in the federation of Europe, and will change the destinies of those regions which have long been devoted to the manufacture of munitions of war, of which they have been the most constant victims."

THE Benelux countries were among those which responded to Schuman's proposal although, like Germany and Italy, which also showed interest in the French idea, they had some reservations about its radical element—the supranational High Authority. Negotiations were tedious and involved, but Schuman later recalled them in a bright light. "The six delegations," he said, "were in some sense allies, pooling their knowledge and their goodwill."

Whatever the economic motives or the specifics which had to be worked out, the delegates saw in Schuman's proposal a step toward the kind of cooperation which might help to prevent the disasters of the war they had just endured. A treaty establishing the Coal and Steel Community was signed on April 18, 1951, and was ratified by the parliaments of the six member nations by the following summer. Not long afterward the High Authority of the

Community held its first meeting, with representatives from each country participating and with Jean Monnet as president. In February 1953, duties, restrictions, dual pricing and transport discriminations on coal, iron ore and scrap were eliminated. Steel followed the next year.

This common market for coal and steel showed what was possible by economic union. By 1958, the year established as the end of the initial transition period, employment in the Community's coal and steel industries had risen by 80,000, and earnings had increased 21 per cent. Coke, iron ore, pig iron and steel production climbed while prices were kept fairly level. Only coal suffered, a result of the inroads made by oil, methane and natural gas in Europe.

THE success of the Coal and Steel Community inspired ideas for supranational authorities in other fields. Most of these, however, proved abortive. S. L. Mansholt, the Dutch Minister of Agriculture, suggested a European Agricultural Community; Edouard Bonnefous, a member of the French parliament, proposed a European Transport Organization; Paul Ribeyre, the French minister of health, sought a European Health Community. A proposed European Defense Community was defeated by the French Assembly in 1954. That year, as if in reaction to this blow, the Common Assembly of the Coal and Steel Community established a committee to examine the possibilities of extending the Community's activities in the economic area. In June 1955 the foreign ministers of the Community's member states heard several suggestions. The first and most important came from the Benelux countries, which by then were beginning to see palpable benefits from their expanding economic integration.

"The moment has come," the Benelux message read, "to pass into a new stage of European integration . . . this must be achieved first in the economic field." This was more than enough to spur study of the combined proposals at a series of meetings held near Brussels. This committee's report was adopted in May 1956. On March 25, 1957, treaties were signed in Rome which established the European Atomic Energy Community (Euratom) and the European Economic Community (Common Market, or Euromart as some Europeans prefer). By the end of the year, the treaties were ratified, and on January 1, 1958, they came into force.

Euratom's concern is not with armaments but with the peaceful uses of atomic energy. Its premise was that over the long haul, oil and coal would be replaced as sources of power and that its member nations were far behind the United States, Russia and Great Britain in nuclear research. Financial problems have kept Euratom from moving as vigorously as some of its leaders would have liked. By mid-1961 a power program in collaboration with the United States was under way, but it provided for only 1.5 million kilowatts of power capacity with the hope that this would reach two million kilowatts by 1965; Euratom officials had hoped for 15 million by 1967, a goal now conceded to be unattainable.

Despite the disappointment, research continues, safety standards have been established for member nations and a team of inspectors is employed to see that Euratom's nuclear materials are not employed for military uses. The controls are so respected that the United States supplies Euratom with fissionable materials without insisting on inspections by American officials.

THE Common Market at present is essentially a customs union of the Benelux countries plus France, Italy and Germany. Its goals are similar to those of Benelux—complete freedom for the movement of goods, manpower and capital within the area. When the Market was established, its program called for the abolition of tariff walls between the member nations; tariffs to nonmember nations were to be averaged out and commonly applied.

Tariffs, however, have not been the only barriers raised against trade among nations over the years. Quantitative restrictions on imports, a traditional device to protect home industries, had to be equalized among the members. Even harder to erase have been the subtler means nations have used for protection of native industries—subsidies, for example, which put local manufacturers or farmers in a better competitive situation than their foreign counterparts. Taxes, freight charges and unrealistic quality standards have also been used to discourage foreign competition. Some countries used to add loading and unloading charges at frontiers whether or not trains were stopped. The purpose of the Common Market from its inception was to remove all such barriers to a true union. Realistically, the officials of the Common Market understood that such an achievement would take time. A specific timetable for reductions was established so that everyone involved knew exactly where he stood. Twelve years—or 1970—was set as the target date, but indications are that the industrial goals will be reached by 1967 or even sooner.

AS the final date approaches, the Benelux countries—which still have their own union within the larger one—have begun to feel the impact of the Common Market. Because Brussels is the headquarters for Euratom and the Common Market, Belgium has had to adjust to more obvious changes than Holland has. Some 4,000 Common Market employees live in the city, and some of them have even taken to referring to it as the capital of Europe. Unlike Holland, Belgium had the facilities to take care of this invasion, and it even seems to enjoy its new role in European affairs.

On a practical level—which Belgians generally reach sooner or later—the Common Market has meant an expansion of industries which were once purely local. A new industrial park near the town of Mons will house factories turning out products for other members of the Common Market as well as for Belgium. Properly enough for beer-loving Belgium, one of the first Mons plants was a brewery. "Now one or two million people in northern France who have nothing but wine to drink can get our really good Belgian beer," explained Governor Émile Cornez of Hainaut province. In Holland, products from France, Italy and Germany which were once outrageously expensive are now available at prices that the middle classes, at least, can afford.

THE feeling in the Low Countries, as reflected by the press and government and business leaders, is one of optimism about the future of the Common Market, and now that the painful years have passed, of Benelux as well. Nevertheless there are many difficulties ahead. Symbolic of them is the problem of the butter smugglers along the Dutch-Belgian border. The best guess today is that some 12 million pounds of Dutch butter are brought into Belgium illegally each year by smugglers who brave rivers, border guards and other vicissitudes to achieve their goal—annual profits running to about one million dollars.

No one seems to know how to stop the smuggling. Butter prices are subsidized in Holland, and butter is sold there for the equivalent of 50 cents a pound. A Belgian housewife or restaurant owner, on the other hand, pays 80 cents a pound because the Belgian government, to protect local farmers, keeps the price up by regulating imports.

The Dutch do not feel they can do anything about the situation. If they permitted the sale price of butter to rise to the Belgian level, and thus ruined the smuggling industry, Dutch housewives would be outraged. Moreover, a rise in the price of butter could push up the Dutch cost-of-living index, which would cause a wage rise. Dutch officials consider it a lot simpler and cheaper to pay the $60 million to $140 million annual subsidy to dairymen and to suffer Belgian complaints.

It is unlikely that Benelux will collapse over butter. Butter is simply one of the slippery hazards on the road to integration which the engineers of a united Europe may have foreseen, but could not have avoided.

Eager brokers at the Brussels stock exchange crowd around a "corbeille," or metal basket, where several active stocks are being traded.

Sturdy Economies Spurred by Growing Trade

The economies of the Low Countries have made amazing gains since World War II. Now they look forward to great prosperity through the Common Market. As tariff barriers fall, their steels, textiles and other products are finding buyers all over Europe, and their ports, canals and railways are busier than ever. A sign of things to come is the fact that Brussels, housing the Common Market's executive body, is already being called the "Capital of Europe."

INDUSTRIAL GIANT of the Netherlands is Philips Industries with 13 separate divisions

MASTERMINDS of Philips' complex operations, Frits Philips *(left)*, current president, and Frans Otten, his predecessor, watch a Philips-backed team play soccer.

Obtaining vaccine, technicians gather influenza virus from infected eggs at Philips-Duphar, the company's medical supply branch.

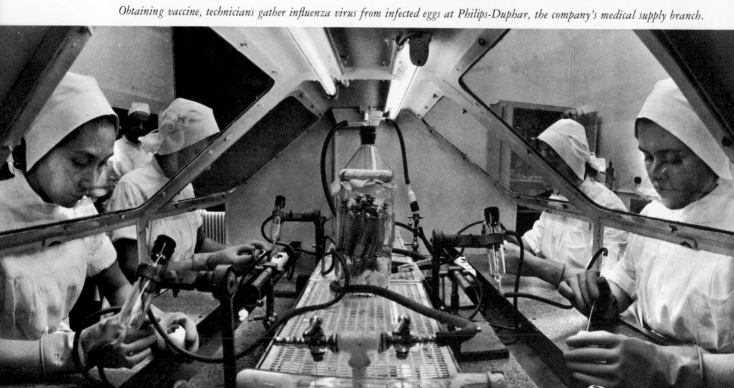

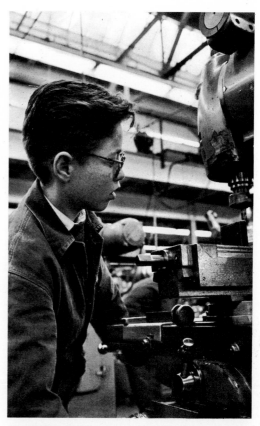

AN APPRENTICE, 13-year-old Johan Possmans learns glass-instrument-making at the Philips training school, where some 1,200 students are taught industrial skills.

MASS PRODUCTION of television tubes *(left)* has helped make Philips a leading manufacturer of television sets. The company has pioneered in electronics research.

Researchers observe the growth of young apple trees in the rigidly controlled climate of a greenhouse at Philips' biological laboratory.

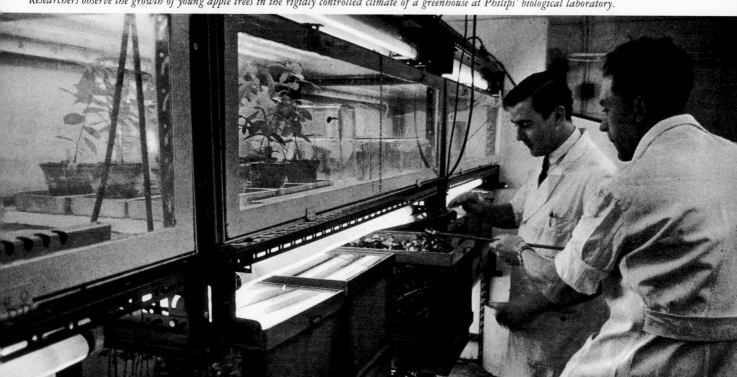

GREAT MILLS overshadow the town of Esch-sur-Alzette, the center of Luxembourg's steel industry. Despite its small size, Luxembourg is one of the largest steel producers in the world.

PROSPEROUS WORKERS ride motorbikes *(right)* through the gate of a large steelworks in Athus, Belgium. Belgium's heavy industry is concentrated between Liège and the French border.

DAIRY FARMERS crowd the square before the 15th Century Dutch town hall of Gouda to sell their big "wheels" of Gouda cheese. Holland exports 250 million pounds of cheese a year.

THE RICH LAND is still painstakingly

GRAPE PICKERS fill conical buckets with wine grapes *(left)* at a Moselle River vineyard in Luxembourg. The white wines of Luxembourg are esteemed for their delicacy and dryness.

POTATO DIGGERS fill their baskets on a farm in Luxembourg's principal agricultural area, called the *Bon Pays*, or good country, a fertile lowland plain south of the Ardennes plateau. Luxembourg's farms are generally small, averaging about 30 acres, and the soil is sandy, but with fertilizer and determined hard work the farmers manage to raise a wide variety of crops.

10

A Community of Nations

DESIDERIUS ERASMUS, the great 16th Century humanist who was one of the world's first internationalists, once wrote to a friend: "That you are patriotic will be praised by some and easily forgotten by everyone; but in my opinion it is wiser to treat men and things as though we held this world the common fatherland of all." Since the prospects for world unity are, at the moment, rather bleak, the only apparent hope for complying with the Erasmus dictum is in the movement now under way to achieve at least a common fatherland for Europe. The Dutch, the Belgians and the Luxembourgers were among the first to realize

that the Common Market might serve as a steppingstone toward eventual European political unity. What is more, in the tradition of Erasmus, they were in favor of taking the next steps toward that larger unity.

The reasons for Low Countries support of a united Europe are historic and geographic. With the exception of a few periods, history for them has been a relentless series of wars, invasions and occupations. Because of their size, Holland, Belgium and Luxembourg by themselves have had neither the military nor economic power to prevent larger nations from impinging on them. Today they are, by virtue of the atom, in an even weaker position than they were in the periods when Napoleon, the Kaiser and Hitler marched across their lands. If there is safety in numbers, the Low Countries prefer that to going it alone, which they did in World War I with resulting catastrophe for Belgium and Luxembourg, and in World War II with catastrophe for all three of them.

With the passing of their colonies, Holland and Belgium have relinquished dreams of glory. Even before they lost Indonesia, the Dutch knew their place among the nations of the world. A favorite postwar story was that of the two sailors, one Dutch and one English, sitting in a London pub during the blitz. The Englishman gradually grew more and more morose, and the Dutchman asked him the cause of his sadness. The Englishman said, "I just remembered that the Dutch navy once sailed up the Thames." In a few seconds the Dutchman too became sad. The Englishman straightened up and asked the Dutchman the reason for his tears. And the Dutch sailor responded, "Because we'll never do it again."

The knowledge that there are a good many things they will never do again—achieving empires, for example—has led the Dutch and Belgians to concentrate on those things that are within reach. In their case, a larger European market unhampered by trade barriers may prove more beneficial than their colonies ever were. The realization of that fact has led them to an increasing participation in the European economic movement.

GUIDE TO EUROPEAN ASSOCIATIONS

Of the many organizations established to promote European economic unity since World War II, six have become most important:

OECD, the Organization for Economic Cooperation and Development, is an outgrowth of the Organization for European Economic Cooperation, formed in 1948 by the countries participating in the Marshall Plan. Full members now include the U.S., Canada and 18 European nations. The OECD's purpose is to expand economic growth in member countries and extend aid to underdeveloped nations.

ECSC, or the European Coal and Steel Community, was set up in 1952 by the Low Countries and France, Italy and West Germany for the free movement of coal, steel, iron ore and scrap between member states.

EEC, or European Economic Community, also known as the Common Market, is the economic union organized in 1958 by the Low Countries, France, West Germany and Italy.

EURATOM, or the European Atomic Community, was set up by ECSC members in 1958 to develop nuclear power for peaceful uses.

EFTA, or European Free Trade Association, was established in 1959 by Austria, Britain, Denmark, Norway, Portugal, Sweden and Switzerland for the free movement of industrial goods among members.

BENELUX is an economic union set up in 1960 by Belgium, Holland and Luxembourg.

The Dutch and Belgians are, however, under no illusions that economic alliances will solve all their major domestic problems. In Holland, the population increase makes unemployment a genuine threat for the future. Because industrialization has increased so rapidly since the end of the war, there is little unemployment now. But as succeeding generations come of working age, there are not likely to be enough jobs to go around. If, as is anticipated, the Common Market countries inaugurate a free flow of labor among themselves, it may be possible for jobless Dutchmen to find jobs elsewhere. There is, however, no guarantee that this will happen. If unemployment should also strike other Common Market countries, they are not likely to support moves which would have foreign labor competing with their domestic workers. One Market member—Italy—has a chronic unemployment problem.

Nor does there seem any likelihood that the Common Market will solve Belgium's coal problem in a way that will please the Belgians. The closing of Belgian mines, carried out since 1959 in cooperation with the Coal and Steel Community, has cut Belgian coal production by more than six million tons. Recently, domestic demand for coal has increased and the Belgians would like to step up production. But the Coal and Steel Community, looking at the problem from a European, rather than a Belgian, point of view, is concerned with a general oversupply of coal caused by the increased use of oil and gas. Coal and Steel

Community policy is to continue the restriction of Belgian output. A Belgian National Coal Board is working on a counterproposal. The ultimate test may involve the Coal and Steel Community's power to make decisions which seemingly go against a country's self-interest.

DESPITE an awareness that these, among other problems, will remain unresolved in the foreseeable future, a vast majority of the Dutch, the Belgians and the Luxembourgers support the existing economic community. In addition, they look forward to the formation of the political one. Most of the Walloons and Flemings strongly favor European union. Many of them feel that within the larger community, individual groups will stand a better chance of preserving their identities than they do in a small state. In Holland, nearly all Catholics, Protestants and freethinkers, divided though they may be on other matters, are in agreement on a European political union.

To help achieve this political goal, the Low Countries have pushed for expansion of the present membership of the Common Market. They have been advocates of the entry of Great Britain and of eventually including the six other members of the European Free Trade Association, or Outer Seven (Austria, Denmark, Norway, Portugal, Sweden and Switzerland). But with or without England and the other countries, Holland and Belgium generally favor the creation of a strong supranational authority for the political union, such as that which exists in the Coal and Steel Community.

They believe that anything less, such as the vesting of control in a body in which members would speak for their own countries and a rule of unanimity would prevail, would put small nations at a disadvantage. Paul-Henri Spaak summed up the Low Countries position recently. "I have always opposed what people call the 'Europe des Patries' [Europe of Fatherlands]," he said. "I consider this idea to be inadequate and inefficient. The unanimity rule leads us finally into the situation in which the stubborn attitude of one country makes the majority accept the policy of the minority."

Given Europe's tradition of nationalism, the attitude of the Low Countries is exceedingly bold. But the groundwork for larger union is being strengthened nearly every day by the Common Market's executive body, a nine-man commission composed of two Frenchmen, two Germans, two Italians, one Belgian, one Dutchman and one Luxembourger. These men sit as individuals, not as representatives of their various governments. Staff members—more than one fourth of them are from the Low Countries —are strongly dedicated to the European ideal, and promote it vigorously.

Some of the regulations issued by the Common Market Commission already have the same force of law in European courts as domestic legislation. Although the commission sometimes acts as if it were in fact a government, its members are aware of the precedents they are establishing and of the need to move carefully. As a result of one agricultural decision, for instance, French and Italian grapes started to flood the Belgian market at prices much cheaper than those of domestic grapes. When the harmful effect of this decision on Belgian grape growers was shown, the commission permitted Belgium briefly to suspend imports.

AS conscious as it may be of local hardships which may arise in connection with its decisions, the commission is proceeding to delve into areas once deemed purely of national interest. It is determined to prevent private agreements "which have as their object or result the prevention, restriction or distortion of competition within the Common Market." Such agreements, a euphemism for the cartel arrangements which were once so prominent a part of the European economy, are being examined to see whether they result in price fixing, market sharing or other practices now illegal under Common Market law.

A body becoming increasingly influential in Western Europe is the Court of Justice, which meets in Luxembourg. The court is empowered to "ensure observance of law and justice in the interpretation and application" of the treaties which established the Common Market, Euratom and the Coal and Steel Community, collectively known as the European Community. In its short life the court has already made decisions cutting across national boundaries, and many more such judgments are on the way. Once the court accelerates the crackdown on cartels that it has already begun, it will become a busy place. Nobody can predict how far this process will go, but the court has been granted a wide scope. It may take action on appeals by a member country, by institutions or officials of the Community and even on appeals by private firms or associations.

There is, of course, opposition to the concept of a supranational European union advocated by Low Countries leaders. Of these opposing voices, the most formidable has been that of President Charles de Gaulle of France. "Would the French people, the German people, the Italian people, the Dutch people, the Belgian people, the Luxembourg people," De Gaulle has asked, "be ready to submit to laws voted by strangers when these laws ran contrary to their deepest will?" Rather than a supranational European union, De Gaulle apparently envisions a multinational European community, economically integrated to an extent, but one in which each nation would continue to play its individual role. In short, he appears to want the "Europe of Fatherlands" which the Low Countries emphatically do not want.

IN the Low Countries, there remains a conviction that "the strengthening of world peace that would result from a European community in which no member could [dominate] the others," as President John F. Kennedy of the United States expressed it in 1962, has priority over all issues. Young people especially have urged swifter action toward political union. They see in it the strongest hope for avoiding the rivalries of their elders which led to two major wars. A sense of being Europeans first, and Dutchmen, Belgians or Luxembourgers second, has been growing.

Nationalism is not expected to die, of course, but there are signs that it has suffered some wounds. Among the achievements of the European Community has been the establishment of four international schools. Although originally conceived for the education of children of Community staff members, they are now open to all children, regardless of nationality. The school in Brussels has pupils from some 20 countries, but the matter of nationality does not appear to carry much weight with the children. Recently, an eight-year-old started classes in mid-term. During recess, a teacher overheard a classmate ask the newcomer where she was from. "Euratom," said the young lady.

ONLY the most starry-eyed idealist can foresee a day when regional or national differences will entirely disappear. Those who favor European political union do not anticipate that. They are ready to settle for the promise held out by Winston Churchill, that early advocate of Western unity, in 1946. "If Europe is to be saved from infinite misery, and indeed from final doom," Churchill said, "there must be an act of faith in the European family and an act of oblivion against all the crimes and follies of the past. . . . What is this sovereign remedy? It is to re-create the European family . . . and to provide it with a structure under which it can dwell in peace, safety, and freedom. We must build a kind of United States of Europe. . . ."

Whether the European community that is now evolving will pattern itself after the United States of America or will take another form—perhaps one better suited to European needs—is not very important. What has been achieved since the end of the war is remarkable by any measure. It is possible that given years of peace and good will and an incredible amount of hard work, the union of Europe that was never attained by armies may be created by some hardheaded men who leave national interests behind when they come to work at the Common Market's offices on the Avenue of the Joyeuse Entrée, Brussels.

School children in Brussels cross a boulevard with their teacher. Next page: Dutch girls arrive in Amsterdam for a class reunion.

LOOKING FORWARD *to the day when their small nations become parts . . .*

. . . of a united Europe, the young people of the Low Countries are confident that,

profiting from their ancestors' experience, they can help construct a new world

Appendix

HISTORICAL DATES

B.C.

57 Julius Caesar conquers tribes he calls the Belgae in areas now a part of the Low Countries

15 These areas become the imperial Roman province of Gallia Belgica. Latin and Roman law take root

A.D.

69-71 Julius Civilis leads dissident Batavi tribesmen in a futile revolt against the Romans

3rd Century Roman power declines as Franks, Germanic tribes and the sea invade Gallia Belgica from all sides. Waters wash over the northern marshlands and form the Zuiderzee

481-511 Clovis, the Frankish king, establishes a state out of the ruins of Roman Gaul. His realm includes parts of the Low Countries

695 Bishopric of Utrecht is founded. Christianity spreads rapidly in the southern regions of the Low Countries, but a firmly entrenched paganism slows its progress in the northern areas

8th Century Systematic dike-building begins in Friesland

721 Bishopric of Liège is established

768-814 Under Charlemagne, the Low Countries are unified to a degree and enjoy a brief period of peace

9th Century Viking invasions end the peace. Floods inundate low-lying coastal regions

843 Areas of the Low Countries are divided among the grandsons of Charlemagne

10th-14th Centuries Small, autonomous principalities, which eventually become Dutch and Belgian provinces, emerge and challenge the suzerainty of French and German monarchs. Cities, particularly in Flanders, gain increasing power and wealth from their textile industries and trade

1384-1455 Philip the Bold and succeeding dukes of Burgundy gradually gain possession of or influence over most areas of the Low Countries

1477 On the death of the last Burgundian duke, the Low Countries pass to the Austrian House of Hapsburg

1519-1556 Reign of Holy Roman Emperor Charles V, born at Ghent. He organizes the Low Countries into the "Seventeen Provinces" of the Netherlands

1522 Charles utilizes the Inquisition to discourage Protestantism, but Lutheranism and Calvinism draw many converts

1556-1568 Charles's son, Philip II of Spain, inherits the Netherlands. He sends the Duke of Alba there to enforce discipline and halt the heresies. Alba earns the title of "the Bloody Duke"

1568 The Eighty Years' War begins. William the Silent, Prince of Orange, leads a resistance army against Spanish rule in the "Beggars Revolt"

1576-1579 Pacification of Ghent. The provinces unite briefly, but the Catholic southern provinces (roughly, modern Belgium and Luxembourg), fearful of Calvinist growth, break with the northern and conclude a separate peace with Spain

1579-1581 Seven Protestant provinces in the north form the United Provinces of the Netherlands and issue a declaration of independence from Spain

1584-1609 William the Silent is assassinated in Delft. His sons and grandson carry on the war

17th Century Golden age of the Netherlands. Painting reaches its zenith in the Low Countries. Despite religious and political conflicts, the Netherlands becomes a leading industrial and maritime power and begins colonial expansion in Asia and the Americas

1648 Peace of Westphalia. European powers recognize the independence of the Netherlands. The Belgian provinces remain under Spanish governors

1702-1713 War of the Spanish Succession. At its end, the Belgian provinces are placed under the rule of the Austrian Hapsburgs

1702-1792 Trade and culture decline in the Netherlands. Its sea power is destroyed by England during the American Revolution. Political strife keeps the country on the verge of civil war

1715-1748 The Dutch, British and French squeeze the Belgian provinces out of commercial competition. The territory again serves as a battleground in the War of the Austrian Succession

1780-1790 Emperor Joseph II pushes too many reforms on traditional-minded Belgians. They form a republic but fail to unite behind it, and Austria resumes control

1795 After invasion by French revolutionary forces, the Netherlands becomes the Batavian Republic and a satellite of France

1796 The Belgian provinces are incorporated into the French First Republic

1806 Napoleon creates the Kingdom of Holland and places his brother Louis on its throne

1810 Napoleon forces Louis' abdication and annexes the kingdom to his French Empire

1815 After Napoleon's defeat at Waterloo, the southern and northern provinces are united as the Kingdom of the Netherlands under William I of Orange

1830 The Belgians revolt and declare Belgium an independent constitutional monarchy

1831 Leopold I, Prince of Saxe-Coburg, is chosen as King of the Belgians

1867 An international conference called to settle a Dutch, French and Prussian quarrel over Luxembourg, grants it independence as the Grand Duchy of Luxembourg

1876-1885 Belgium's King Leopold II gains control and is named sovereign of the Independent State of the Congo

1908 The Congo becomes a Belgian colony

1914-1918 World War I. Germany invades Belgium and Luxembourg. The Netherlands remains neutral

1920 Draining of Zuiderzee begins

1921 The Belgium-Luxembourg Economic Union (BLEU) is formed

1940-1945 World War II. Belgium's King Leopold II surrenders to the invading Germans and is interned. Dutch and Luxembourg governments go into exile in Britain

1944 Representatives in exile of all three countries draft a common customs agreement

1948 Juliana ascends the Dutch throne

1949 The Low Countries join the North Atlantic Treaty Organization (NATO). The Netherlands recognizes Indonesian independence

1951 Baudouin ascends the Belgian throne

1958 The three countries become members of the Common Market and the European atomic energy organization (EURATOM)

1960 Belgium recognizes independence of the Congo

152

FOR FURTHER READING

CHAPTER 1: UNITY AND DIVERSITY

Barnouw, Adriaan J., *The Dutch*. Columbia University Press, 1940.

Eyck, F. Gunther, *The Benelux Countries: An Historical Survey*. Anvil, 1959.

Goris, Jan-Albert, ed., *Belgium*. University of California Press, 1945.

Landheer, Bartholomeus, ed., *The Netherlands*. University of California Press, 1943.

Petit, Joseph, *Luxembourg, Yesterday and Today*. P. Linden, Luxembourg.

Schoenen, Paul, *Belgium*. Helicon Press, 1955.

CHAPTER 2: YEARS OF TURBULENCE

Barnouw, Adriaan J., *The Making of Modern Holland*. W. W. Norton, 1944.

Clough, Shepard B., *The History of the Flemish Movement; A Study in Nationalism*. Farrar & Rinehart, 1930.

Edler, Friedrich, *The Dutch Republic and the American Revolution*. Johns Hopkins, 1911.

Geyl, Pieter, *The Revolt of the Netherlands*. Barnes & Noble, 1958. *The Netherlands in the 17th Century*. Barnes & Noble, 1961.

Huizinga, Johan, *The Waning of the Middle Ages*. Doubleday, 1954.

Meeüs, Adrien de, *History of the Belgians*. Frederick A. Praeger, 1962.

Motley, John Lothrop, *The Rise of the Dutch Republic*. 3 vols., E. P. Dutton, 1906.

Van Loon, Hendrik Willem, *The Rise of the Dutch Kingdom*. Doubleday, Page, 1915.

Vlekke, Bernard H. M., *Evolution of the Dutch Nation*. Roy Publishers, 1945.

Wedgwood, C. V., *William the Silent; William of Nassau, Prince of Orange, 1533-1584*. Yale University Press, 1944.

CHAPTER 3: THE TOPPLED EMPIRES

Goris, Jan-Albert, *Belgium in Bondage*. L. B. Fischer, 1943.

Hennessy, Maurice N., *The Congo; A Brief History of Appraisal*. Frederick A. Praeger, 1961.

Hyma, Albert, *The History of the Dutch in the Far East*. G. Wahr, 1953.

Jong, Louis de, and Joseph W. F. Stoppelman, *The Lion Rampant*. Querido, 1943.

Luxembourg and the German Invasion, Before and After. Hutchinson, 1942.

Mintz, Jeanne S., *Indonesia; A Profile*. D. Van Nostrand, 1961.

Motz, Roger, *Belgium Unvanquished*. L. Drummond, London, 1942.

Palmier, Leslie H., *Indonesia and the Dutch*. Oxford University Press, 1962.

Poll, Willem van de, *The Netherlands West Indies*. W. Van Hoeve, The Hague, 1951.

Riemens, Hendrik, *The Netherlands, Story of a Free People*. Duell, Sloan & Pearce, 1944.

Slade, Ruth, *King Leopold's Congo*. Oxford University Press, 1962.

Vlekke, Bernard H. M., *Nusantara; A History of Indonesia*. Quadrangle Books, 1960.

CHAPTER 4: THE ROYAL DEMOCRACIES

Barnouw, Adriaan J., *The Pageant of Netherlands History*. Longmans, Green, 1952.

Cammaerts, Emile, *History of the Belgian Dynasty*. Peter Davies, London, 1939.

Lichtervelde, Louis de, *Leopold of the Belgians*. Century, 1929.

CHAPTER 5: OUT OF THE RUBBLE

Landheer, Bartholomeus, *The Netherlands in a Changing World; A Series of Essays*. Roy Publishers, 1947.

Mumford, Lewis, *The City in History*. Harcourt, Brace & World, 1961.

Roberts, Katharine, *And the Bravest of These*. Doubleday, 1946.

Roosenburg, Henriette, *The Walls Came Tumbling Down*. Viking Press, 1957.

CHAPTER 6: LITERATURE AND THE ARTS

Boswell, James. *Boswell in Holland, 1763-1764*. Frederick A. Pottle, ed., McGraw-Hill, 1952.

Delta; A Review of Arts, Life and Thought in the Netherlands. Delta International Foundation, Amsterdam.

Dubois, Pierre H., *Dutch Art Today; Literature*. Contact, Amsterdam, 1956.

Frank, Anne, *The Diary of a Young Girl*. Modern Library, 1952.

Greshoff, Jan, ed., *Harvest of the Lowlands*. Querido, 1945.

Herbert, Eugenia W., *The Artist and Social Reform: France and Belgium, 1885-1898*. Yale University Press, 1961.

Janson, H. W., *History of Art*. Harry N. Abrams, 1962.

Konigsberger, Hans, *Modern Dutch Painting*. Netherlands Information Service, 1954.

Lassaigne, Jacques, *Flemish Painting*. Vol. 1, Skira, Geneva, 1957. With Robert L. Delevoy, *Flemish Painting*. Vol. 2, 1958.

Leymarie, Jean, *Dutch Painting*. Skira, Geneva, 1956.

Ninane, Lucie, and others. *Flanders in the Fifteenth Century: Art and Civilization*.

Wayne State University Press, 1960.

"Perspective of Holland and Belgium." An *Atlantic* supplement. April 1954.

Romein-Verschoor, A., *Silt and Sky; Men and Movements in Modern Dutch Literature*. Em. Querido, Amsterdam, 1950.

Timmers, J.J.M., *History of Dutch Life and Art*. Thomas Nelson, 1959.

Van Loon, Hendrik Willem, *Rembrandt van Rijn*. Heritage Press, 1944.

Weevers, Theodoor, *Poetry of the Netherlands in Its European Context, 1170-1930*. University of London, 1960.

CHAPTER 7: WATER, WATER, EVERYWHERE

From Fisherman's Paradise to Farmer's Pride. Netherlands Ministry of Transport and Waterstaat, The Hague, 1959.

Graftdijk, Klaas, *Holland Rides the Sea*. World's Window, Baarn, Holland, 1960.

Maris, A. G., ed., *The Dutch and Their Dikes*. De Bezige Bij, Amsterdam, 1956.

Monkhouse, F. J., *A Regional Geography of Western Europe*. Longmans, Green, 1959.

Veen, J. Van, *Dredge, Drain, Reclaim! The Art of a Nation*. Martinus Nijhoff, The Hague, 1950.

CHAPTER 8: PRIDE AND PROVINCIALISM

Glass, David Victor. *Population Policies and Movements in Europe*. Clarendon Press, 1940.

Sitwell, Sacheverell, *The Netherlands: A Study of Some Aspects of Art, Costume and Social Life*. Hastings House, 1955.

Van Paassen, Pierre, *Earth Could Be Fair*. Dial Press, 1946.

CHAPTERS 9 & 10:

THE VANISHING CUSTOMS HOUSE

Belgium-Luxembourg Economic Union. Organization for European Economic Co-operation, Paris, 1960.

Benoit, Emile, *Europe at Sixes and Sevens*. Columbia University Press, 1961.

Customs Union. Department of Economic Affairs. United Nations Publications, 1947.

Deniau, Jean F., *The Common Market*. Frederick A. Praeger, 1960.

Economic Conditions in the Netherlands, 1960. Organization for European Economic Co-operation. Paris, 1960.

Hauser, Rita E. and Gustave M., *A Guide to Doing Business in the Common Market*. Oceana, 1960.

Mayne, Richard, *The Community of Europe*. W. W. Norton, 1962.

Nystrom, J. Warren, and Peter Malof, *The Common Market; The European Community in Action*. D. Van Nostrand, 1962.

FAMOUS LOW COUNTRIES CULTURAL FIGURES AND THEIR PRINCIPAL WORKS

Countries of origin are not given until the 19th Century, when Belgium became an independent nation.

ARCHITECTURE AND SCULPTURE

Sluter, Claus	?-c.1405	The Moses Well at the Chartreuse de Champmol near Dijon
Vriendt, Cornelis de (Floris)	1514-1575	Antwerp Town Hall in Flemish Renaissance style; choir screen in Tournai Cathedral
Crabeth, Dirck	fl.1555-1577	Stained-glass windows in St. Janskerk at Gouda (with his brother, Wouter, and others)
Key, Lieven de	c.1560-1627	Vleeshal (Butchers' Hall) in Haarlem
Keyser, Hendrik de	1565-1621	Zuiderkerk in Amsterdam; the baroque tomb of William the Silent in Delft; towers and gates
Meunier, Constantin	1831-1905	Belgian. Sculptures of coal miners, farmers and factory workers
Berlage, Hendrik	1856-1934	Dutch. Stock Exchange in Amsterdam. He was the first to break with the romantic nationalist traditions of the 19th Century
Velde, Henry van de	1863-1957	Belgian. Rijksmuseum Kröller-Müller in Hoenderloo, Netherlands. He led the *art nouveau* movement in architecture
Minne, Georges	1866-1941	Belgian. One of the *art nouveau* leaders in sculpture

LITERATURE

Veldeke, Hendrik van	12th Century	First known Netherlands poet
Hadewijch	c.1200-c.1269	Religious-mystical lyric poetry
Willem	fl.c.1250	Satirical animal tale: *Van den Vos Reynaerde (Reynard the Fox)*
Maerlant, Jacob van	c.1235-c.1300	Didactic poetry
Ruusbroec, Jan van	1293-1381	Mystical treatises: *The Spiritual Espousals, The Book of the Twelve Béguines*
Anonymous	14th and 15th Centuries	*Beatrijs (Beatrice)* and *Elckerlyc (Everyman)*, legend and play
Thomas à Kempis	c.1380-1471	Religious-mystical treatise: *The Imitation of Christ*
Erasmus, Desiderius	c.1467-1536	Humanist essays: *The Praise of Folly, Colloquies*
Bijns, Anna	1494-1575	Poetry defending Roman Catholic orthodoxy
Marnix van St. Aldegonde	1540-1598	Anti-Catholic treatise: *The Beehive of the Holy Roman Church.* Attributed to him: *Wilhelmus,* now the Dutch national anthem
Cats, Jacob (Father Cats)	1577-1660	Poetry on homely themes and simple people
Hooft, Pieter Cornelisz	1581-1647	History: *Nederlandsche Historien;* lyric poetry, plays
Groot, Hugo de (Grotius)	1583-1645	Principles of international law: *The Law of War and Peace*
Bredero, Gerbrand A.	1585-1618	Play: *De Spaansche Brabander (The Spaniard in Brabant);* poetry
Vondel, Joost van den	1587-1679	Religious and patriotic poetry; Biblical plays: *Lucifer, Gijsbreght van Aemstel*
Huygens, Constantijn	1596-1687	Elegant and witty poetry
Spinoza, Baruch (Benedictus de)	1632-1677	Philosophy. *Ethics, Treatise on the Improvement of Understanding, Letters*
De Ligne, Prince Charles	1735-1814	Essays and memoirs. Wrote in French
Conscience, Hendrik	1812-1883	Belgian. Wrote in Dutch. He inspired the Flemish movement. Historical novel: *The Lion of Flanders*
Dekker, Eduard Douwes (Multatuli)	1820-1887	Dutch. Novel: *Max Havelaar* (advocating colonial administrative reforms); essays
Coster, Charles de	1827-1879	Belgian. Wrote in French. Novel: *Ulenspiegel,* based on local characteristics, history and folklore
Gezelle, Guido	1830-1899	Belgian. Wrote in Dutch. Poetry combining melody and medieval mysticism
Verhaeren, Emile	1855-1916	Belgian. Wrote in French. Poetry: *The Love Poems of Emile Verhaeren;* play: *Helen of Sparta*
Maeterlinck, Maurice	1862-1949	Belgian. Wrote in French. Plays: *The Blue Bird, Pelléas and Mélisande;* poetry, critical essays
Couperus, Louis	1863-1923	Dutch. Novel: *Van Oude Mensen, de Dingen die Vooorbijghaan (Of Old People, the Things that Pass By)*
Gorter, Herman	1864-1927	Dutch. Poetry: *De School der Poëzie* (a collection), *Mei (May)*
Lateur, Frank (Stijn Streuvels)	1871-	Belgian. Writes in Dutch. Novel: *De Vlaschaard (The Flax Field);* short stories
Schendel, Arthur van	1874-1946	Dutch. Novels: *Een Zwerver (A Wanderer), A House in Haarlem, Grey Birds*
Woestijne, Karel van de	1878-1929	Belgian. Wrote in Dutch. Poetry: *Contemporary Flemish Poetry;* critical essays
Roland Holst, Adrianus	1888-	Dutch. Lyric poetry: *Een Winter aan Zee (A Winter at Sea)*
Nijhoff, Martinus	1894-1953	Dutch. Lyric poetry: *Nieuwe Gedichten (New Poems)*
Plisnier, Charles	1896-1952	Belgian. Wrote in French. Short stories: *Faux Passeports (False Passports);* novel: *Mariages (Marriages)*
Ghelderode, Michel de	1898-1962	Belgian. Wrote in French. Plays: *Escurial, Pantagleize, Barabbas*
Vestdijk, Simon	1898-	Dutch. Novel: *Anton Wachter's Jeugd (The Youth of Anton Wachter);* historical novel: *Het Vijfde Zegel (The Fifth Seal);* essays, poetry
Marsman, Hendrik	1899-1940	Dutch. Lyric poetry: *Verzamelde Gedichten (Collected Poems)*
Perron, Charles Edgar du	1899-1940	Dutch. Novel: *Het Land van Herkomst (Homeland);* short stories, essays
Goris, Jan-Albert (Marnix Gijsen)	1899-	Belgian. Writes in Dutch. Novels: *The Book of Joachim of Babylon, Klaaglied om Agnes (Lament for Agnes);* poetry, essays
Braak, Menno ter	1902-1940	Dutch. Essays: *Het Carnaval der Burgers (Bourgeois Carnival), Van Oude en Nieuwe Christenen (Of Old and New Christians)*
Simenon, Georges	1903-	Belgian. Writes in French. Novels and detective stories
Boon, Louis Paul	1912-	Belgian. Writes in Dutch. Novel: *De Kapellekensbaan (Little Chapel Road)*
Hermans, Willem Frederik	1921-	Dutch. Novel: *The Dark Room of Damocles*
Frank, Anne	1929-1945	Dutch. *The Diary of Anne Frank*

MUSIC

Binchois, Gilles (de Binche)	c.1400-1460	Rondeaux: *De plus en plus, Triste plaisir;* hymn: *O solis à marier*
Dufay, Guillaume	c.1400-1474	Masses: *Missa Caput, Missa se la face ay pale;* motets, hymns

Ockeghem, Johannes	c.1420-c.1495	Masses: *Missa Mi-mi, Missa L'Homme Armé;* rondeau: *Fors seulement*
Obrecht, Jacob	1450-1505	Motets: *Parce Domine, Si oblitus fuero*
Prés, Josquin des	c.1450-1521	Motets: *Ave Maria, Miserere, Tribulatio et angustia;* masses: *Missa Pange lingua, Missa De beata Virgine;* songs
Willaert, Adrian	c.1490-1562	Early madrigals, motets, songs
Lassus, Roland de (Orlando di Lasso)	c.1532-1594	*Penitential Psalms, Lamentations, Spiritual Madrigals;* also secular forms
Sweelinck, Jan Pieter	1562-1621	Compositions for organ
Grétry, André	1742-1813	Operas: *Zémire et Azor, Richard Coeur-de-Lion*
Franck, César	1822-1890	Belgian. *Symphony in D Minor, Variations Symphoniques* for piano and orchestra
Pijper, Willem	1894-1947	Dutch. Symphonies, symphonic epigrams; concertos for piano, violin, cello with orchestra; incidental music for the theater
Badings, Henk	1907-	Dutch. *Concerto for Two Violins and Orchestra;* electronic music

PAINTING

Eyck, Hubert van	1366?-1426?	Flemish School. Central panel of the Ghent altarpiece: *The Adoration of the Lamb*
Eyck, Jan van	c.1385-1441	Flemish School. Ghent altarpiece; *Giovanni Arnolfini and His Wife, The Madonna of Chancellor Rolin, The Madonna of the Canon van der Paele*
Flémalle, Master of	fl.1425	Flemish School. Mérode altarpiece; *The Virgin and Child Before a Fire Screen*
Weyden, Rogier van der	1399-1464	Flemish School. Altarpieces: *The Seven Sacraments, The Last Judgment, Bladelin; Portrait of a Young Lady*
Bouts, Dirk	c.1415-1475	Flemish School. Altarpiece: *The Holy Sacrament; The Ordeal by Fire* (second panel of *The Justice of Otto*)
Memling, Hans	c.1433-1494	Flemish School. Paintings on the reliquary of St. Ursula, *Sambetha Sibyl* portrait, *The Passion of Christ*
Ghent, Joos van	c.1435-after 1475	Flemish School. *Calvary* triptych
Goes, Hugo van der	c.1440-1482	Flemish School. Portinari altarpiece: *The Adoration of the Shepherds; The Fall of Man*
Bosch, Hieronymus	c.1450-1516	Flemish School. Fantastic and nightmarish triptychs: *The Last Judgment, The Temptation of St. Anthony, The Garden of Earthly Delights*
Geertgen tot Sint Jans	c.1460-c.1490	Dutch School. *Lamentation of Christ, Story of the Remains of St. John the Baptist*
David, Gerard	c.1460-1523	Flemish School. Altarpiece: *Jean des Trompes; The Annunciation*
Massys, Quentin	1466-1530	Flemish School. *Lamentation over the Dead Christ;* Madonna and Magdalen faces reminiscent of Da Vinci's
Patinir, Joachim	c.1480-1524	Flemish School. *The Flight into Egypt, The Rest on the Flight into Egypt*
Lucas van Leyden	c.1494-1533	Dutch School. Pioneer of genre painting: *The Game of Chess, The Card Players;* triptychs, portraits, etchings
Aertsen, Pieter	1508-1575	Dutch School. Kitchen interiors and peasant scenes: *The Egg Dance*
Bruegel, Pieter	c.1525-1569	Flemish School. Grotesqueries akin to Bosch's, often in protest against Spanish tyranny: *Dulle Griet, The Triumph of Death, The Magpie on the Gallows, The Tower of Babel, Seven Sins* and *Seven Virtues* series
Rubens, Peter Paul	1577-1640	Flemish School. *The Rape of the Daughters of Leucippus, The Fall of the Damned, The Last Judgment, The Adoration of the Magi,* the Medici cycle, portraits, landscapes
Hals, Frans	c.1580-1666	Dutch School. Highly personal portrait style: *Banquet of the Officers of St. George, The Gypsy Girl, Malle Babbe, The Jolly Toper*
Jordaens, Jacob	1593-1678	Flemish School. Merrymaking among the gods and common folk: *Fecundity*
Goyen, Jan van	1596-1679	Dutch School. Poetic land- and seascapes: *Haarlemmer Meer*
Van Dyck, Anthony	1599-1641	Flemish School. Court painter to Charles I of England. Specialized in portraiture
Brouwer, Adriaen	c.1605-1638	Flemish School. Tavern brawls and landscapes: *Card Players, Landscape in Moonlight*
Rembrandt van Rijn	1606-1669	Dutch School. *The Night Watch, The Anatomy Lesson of Professor Tulp, Aristotle Contemplating the Bust of Homer, The Jewish Bride,* portraits, self-portraits, landscapes
Teniers the Younger, David	1610-1690	Flemish School. Genre painting: *Study of Accessories*
Terborch, Gerard	1617-1681	Dutch School. "Satin gown" paintings: *Woman Peeling an Apple, Woman Writing*
Steen, Jan	1626-1679	Dutch School. Lighthearted family scenes: *Merry Company, St. Nicholas' Eve*
Ruisdael, Jacob van	c.1628-1682	Dutch School. Brooding landscapes: *The Jewish Cemetery at Oudekerk, The Windmill at Wijk*
Hooch, Pieter de	1629-c.1684	Dutch School. Cozy interiors and domestic scenes: *The Mother Beside a Cradle, Interior of a Dutch House, A Game of Skittles*
Vermeer, Jan	1632-1675	Dutch School. Silent and intimate subjects, bathed in light: *The Artist in His Studio, The Love Letter;* architecture painting: *Little Street in Delft, View of Delft*
Hobbema, Meindert	1638-1709	Dutch School. Landscapes: *The Avenue, Middelharnis*
Israels, Josef	1824-1911	Dutch. Scheveningen fishermen and the Jewish quarter in Amsterdam
Van Gogh, Vincent	1853-1890	Dutch. Brilliant colors and intensely emotional approach: French landscapes, peasant portraits, self-portraits, still lifes
Toorop, Jan	1858-1928	Dutch. Influenced by mysticism of the Far East
Ensor, James	1860-1949	Belgian. *The Entry of Christ into Brussels;* recurring symbols of masks and skeletons
Mondriaan, Piet	1872-1944	Dutch. Pioneer in *De Stijl* movement; geometric designs in primary colors
Wouters, Rik	1882-1916	Belgian. Dynamic colors and dematerialized forms
Permeke, Constant	1886-1952	Belgian. Expressionism: Flemish peasants and landscapes
Masereel, Frans	1889-	Belgian. Woodcuts: *Passionate Journey; A Novel in 165 Woodcuts*
Delvaux, Paul	1897-	Belgian. Surrealism: *La Prisonnière*
Magritte, René	1898-	Belgian. Surrealism: *The Castle of the Pyrenees, Night at Pisa*

Credits

The sources for the illustrations in this book are shown below. Credits for pictures from left to right are separated by commas, top to bottom by dashes.

Cover—Farrell Grehan

8, 9—Farrell Grehan

12, 13—Maps by Bill Dove

17 through 25—Farrell Grehan

31 through 34—Farrell Grehan

35—Tom Hollyman from Photo Researchers, Inc.

36, 37—Farrell Grehan

38, 39—from *Tempo Doeloe* by E. Breton De Nijs copyright 1961 Em. Querido

41—Courtesy Netherlands Information Service

45—Courtesy Royal Institute for Language Geology and Ethnology from *Tempo Doeloe* by E. Breton De Nijs copyright 1961 Em. Querido

46, 47—Henri Cartier-Bresson from Magnum except left; Wide World Photos

48, 49—Larry Burrows

50, 51—Dmitri Kessel and Yale Joel

57—Courtesy Vlaams Actiecomite, courtesy Mouvement Populaire Wallon

58, 59—Brown Brothers, Dmitri Kessel and Yale Joel, Anpfoto

60, 61—The Bettmann Archive— Pictorial Press from Globe, Gordon Parks, *Paris Match*

62, 63—Dominique Berretty except left; Frank Scherschel

64, 65—Dalmas-Pix—Reporters Associes, Europress-Pix

66, 67—E. J. Marcelis

74—Henk Jonker

75 through 79—Farrell Grehan

80, 81—Henri Cartier-Bresson from Magnum

87—Dmitri Kessel courtesy Royal Museum of Arts, Brussels

88—Courtesy National Gallery, London photo William J. Sumits

89—Raymond and Raymond, Inc. courtesy Staatliche Museen, Berlin-Dahlem— courtesy Samuel H. Kress Memorial Collection, Allentown Art Museum, Allentown, Pennsylvania

90, 91—Courtesy National Gallery, London; Henry B. Beville courtesy Samuel H. Kress Collection in the Seattle Art Museum

92, 93—Courtesy National Gallery, London photo Larry Burrows; courtesy Rijks Museum, Amsterdam

94—Fernand Bourges courtesy Metropolitan Museum of Art, Rogers Fund, 1949

96—Henri Cartier-Bresson from Magnum

101—Map by Bill Dove

103—Drawing by Adolph E. Brotman

105—Carel Blazer

106, 107—Henri Cartier-Bresson from Magnum

108, 109—N. R. Farbman

110, 111—Gordon Tenney, Farrell Grehan

112, 113—Farrell Grehan

119 through 131—Farrell Grehan

137—Tom Hollyman from Photo Researchers, Inc.

138, 139—Stan Wayman

140 through 151—Farrell Grehan

ACKNOWLEDGMENTS

The editors of this book express their appreciation to E. Clark Stillman, President of the Belgian-American Educational Foundation, who read and commented on portions of the text.

Index

This symbol in front of a page number indicates a photograph or painting of the subject mentioned.

Production staff for Time Incorporated

Arthur R. Murphy Jr. (Vice President and Director of Production)

Robert E. Foy, James P. Menton and Caroline Ferri

Text photocomposed under the direction of

Albert J. Dunn and Arthur J. Dunn

x

Printed by R. R. Donnelley & Sons Company, Crawfordsville, Indiana

and The Safran Printing Company, Detroit, Michigan

Bound by R. R. Donnelley & Sons Company, Crawfordsville, Indiana

Paper by The Mead Corporation, Dayton, Ohio